PAGANISM AND THE OCCULT

Paganism and the Occult

KEVIN LOGAN

KINGSWAY PUBLICATIONS
EASTBOURNE

Biblical quotations are from the
New International Version, copyright
© International Bible Society 1973, 1978, 1984.

Front cover photo: Susan Griggs Ltd

British Library Cataloguing in Publication Data

Logan, Kevin
    Paganism and the occult.
    1. Occultism – Christian viewpoints
    2. Paganism
    I. Title
    133

    ISBN 0–86065–628–4

Printed in Great Britain for
KINGSWAY PUBLICATIONS LTD
Lottbridge Drove, Eastbourne, E. Sussex BN23 6NT by
Richard Clay Ltd, Bungay, Suffolk.
Typeset by J&L Composition Ltd., Filey, North Yorkshire

Contents

Acknowledgements

I wanted to mention each of my helpers by name, but the list runs to more than a hundred. To all who have made this book possible my thanks, especially the many prayer warriors without whom I would not have attempted this work. A special thanks to the leaders of St. John's Church, Great Harwood, Lancashire, who allowed me an easy summer to write, and also to Keith and Aileen Nicoll who took the brunt of the work. A tribute is due to the members and ministers of Hyndburn Christian Fellowship and the Northern Evangelical Trust (NET) for their spiritual support and encouragement. My family deserve a medal from heaven for putting up with all the weird happenings which prefaced and accompanied the writing of this book.

It was after a BBC–2 'Open Space' programme entitled 'Lucifer over Lancashire' in April 1987 that I was invited to write this book. The TV documentary focused on a book,[1] published by Hyndburn Christian Fellowship,[2] which highlighted how God had been working in great ways in and around Pendle – the 'occult capital of the North'.

Despatches from the 'frontline' in Lancashire and many other parts of the country, make up a large part of this present book. We are surrounded by more than 30 witches' covens in North-east Lancashire plus an unknown number

7

of other occult groups. The occult affects a significant part of normal ministry for myself and other church leaders in the area, and we have had to deal with the growing number of confused and depressed victims.

As I write, a Member of Parliament[3] is preparing a motion calling on the House of Commons to outlaw witchcraft which, he claims, 'is sweeping the nation' (Hansard, April 14, 1988). It is, of course, an exaggeration, though the statement is not devoid of some truth. There is sympathy when we see certain forms of witchcraft and satanism abusing children – sexually, emotionally and spiritually. When the evidence demands it, I believe that the law must act forcefully. But I readily acknowledge that only a minority within paganism and the occult are breaking the present-day law. I have no wish to inspire witch-hunts nor to reintroduce the village ducking stool. I simply wish to warn people that dabbling in the occult and following pagan practices are dangerous exercises. People who do so are playing with forces which they will be able neither to understand nor control.

Kevin Logan

Introduction

Paganism is the abyss into which man falls when he lets go of God. It is the black hole of man's inner space; a mental, mysterious and magical vortex in which reality must always surrender to fantasy. Time, space and reason distort and warp as modern men and women throw themselves into the void of unknowing. Here only darkness enfolds the mind, and the quest for enlightenment becomes a religion. This internal shadowland of hidden things – the sphere of the occult – is increasingly the destination for twentieth-century humanity. This inner black hole draws with a magnetism which natural man finds hard to resist: it offers that for which he naturally yearns.

'There is no God!' is the cry now reaching a crescendo from many people. 'You are your god! You are a spark of the cosmic deity. Only within is your altar, nature is your temple, and the universal force is the true focus of worship.'

The pagans of old believed no different, until Christianity identified their feared universal force as an all-loving, purposeful personality. The modern-day pagans – disenchanted refugees fleeing an alien era of plastic and silicon chips – have lost the personality, and have reverted back to the force.

To the Victims

As Christians we need to reach out to the victims with love. Christ commissioned his lightbearers to shine into this sombre land of shadows, and this book is an attempt to recharge Christians' batteries, and equip them for this labour of love. I also offer this book as a 'compass' for those lost in the confusion of the occult.

I have avoided the use of emotive language which might prove insensitive and offensive to those on the fringe of the occult. It is written with love to those who might be prepared to open up their minds to the Christian alternative.

The kind of love I mean, however, needs to be unwrapped and understood.

Love is an illusive quality in a selfish, superficial world. Today, it is almost invariably exchanged for words like tolerance, broad-mindedness, indulgence, permissiveness and compromise. It is often difficult to determine whether this kind of loving is aimed at the other person, or whether it is a cheaply disguised self-love yearning for an easy-going, non-critical lifestyle. The love of which I write is the love of God, and not too many are switched on to this. Communicating this kind of loving is rather like broadcasting on VHF while the majority are tuned to medium wave.

What is God's love like? A never-say-die love: God promises to love us from here to eternity. He is love, and he can be no other. It is more an act of the will rather than of feelings.

A forgiving love: it is easy to lose count of the number of times Israel was excused, despite 'her' constant love affairs with pagan gods. At one point, Jeremiah fumes because God's love stretches like everlasting elastic. The prophet demands to know when God is going to stop forgiving the nation's unjust profiteers (Jeremiah 12:1–4).

An all-giving love: from creation to the cross of Calvary and beyond to a new eternal life for all who wish it.

A stern kind of loving: yes, the love of God is eternal, forgiving and all-giving. It is, however, also stern. This is the face of love which few recognise today. God's love is not the slushy, sob-sob kind framed with mist and roses on cinema celluloid. It is a disciplining love that sometimes hurts so that it might help. It was this love that often chastised Israel. This love eventually ensured that God's elastic patience snapped, bringing just but severe punishment on his beloved people, even to the extent of banishing them from the promised homeland. The main theme of the Old Testament shows that God's love spanks rather than spoils. It is a love that seeks the best for the beloved.

To pagans with love – this therefore is our commission, just as it was in the New Testament times.

Paganism and the occult

A pagan, according to the dictionary, is anyone who does not follow one of the main 'one-God' religions, such as Christianity, Judaism or Islam. The word literally means 'a country dweller' or a heathen who has no recognised religion. However, historians and archeologists inform us that they have yet to discover a race or tribe without some form of religion. The Bible, God's definitive dictionary, reinforces this. Scripture makes it clear that man, designed as a worshipping creature, will make up his own belief when God's truth is either ignored or not available to him. The result is always paganism, the attempt to explain that which is hidden, mysterious, supernatural, magical or beyond man's normal senses.

The Bible itself defines paganism without using the word. Paul was inspired to write that men and women will either worship the Creator or that which is created. The pagan suffers from spiritual short-sightedness. He sees no further than nature (Romans 1:25).

The occult comes from the Latin word 'occulta' meaning

'hidden things'. It is the study of the secret, the invisible and the esoteric. Originally, the occult was used to describe a respectable group of academics or students in ancient Mystery centres. Fred Gettings, in his 'Encyclopaedia of the Occult', adds,

> Unfortunately, the use of the term has in recent years become more slipshod, and is now widely applied to virtually any study of unusual phenomena, from psychic experiences in seances to black magic, both areas of human interest which the true occultists would have rejected as being involved with the degradation of humanity or, more simply, as being immoral.

In theory, it is possible to separate paganism and the occult by dictionary definitions. In everyday practice, the two are so closely interwoven that it would be a pedantic, hairsplitting exercise to try to keep them apart. The overlap between the two is too great. Dedicated occultists do, however, object to being labeled as pagans, insisting instead that they are atheists. They also point out that paganism describes the 'unenlightened' and that the occult is primarily concerned with providing enlightenment. However, I have yet to meet a pure, undiluted atheist who, when pushed, does not retreat into uncertain agnosticism. Secondly, the main thesis of this book is that enlightenment is the last thing which the occult provides.

I

The Panorama of Paganism

It was five minutes to a special midnight. Hogmanay pipes
skirled from the television. My normally reserved English
youth fellowship, liberated by gallons of fruit punch and
fortified by cocktail-stick party pickings, swirled in a
Scottish reel, and I began to suspect that the punch had been
spiked! The revelry almost drowned out the shrill of the
amplified vicarage telephone.

'Hello, and a happy New Year!' I sang into the handset.

'Father, it's Gordon from t' club. Can you come quick?'

An urgent fear emphasised the Lancashire accent, and I
resisted the temptation to correct the unbiblical title. I tried
desperately to put a face to the slightly-slurred voice.

'Look, Father, all hell's let loose here. My son's terrifying
the whole family!'

'I'll be with you in two minutes, Gordon,' I said, adopting
a confident-vicar voice, but still trying to recall a face from
the sea which usually greeted me on my casual pastoral visits
to the local working men's club. 'What's your address?'

I dashed out with a hurried explanation, and my startled
wife, I later learned, press-ganged the youth into an emergency prayer meeting. It was certainly needed.

The chimes of the New Year had long faded as I stood at
the bottom of a steep staircase watching the antics of a

pathetic 'spectre' on a dimly-lit landing. The figure, draped in a grubby white bedsheet and producing weird noises straight from the soundtrack of *Ghostbusters*, was the son of the now-remembered Gordon.

I had arrived twenty minutes earlier to be told that the lad had gone out. It had given me time gently to question the distraught mother and to discover that her normally introvert, slightly-built son had become involved with satanists the previous summer. By Christmas, the satanists had left town, abandoning the teenager to his own hell of nightmare visions and nocturnal torments. During those six months, the lad had acted as 'frontman' for the gang's eerie escapades and had been arrested twice. On both occasions he had been sent to Risley Remand Centre at Warrington for psychiatric reports, each time securing a clean bill of mental health. In the light of the son's subsequent behaviour, it was a vital piece of information. I had also been careful to check and rule out the effects of drugs and drink. As I stood looking up at the pitiable wraith – he had apparently been in hiding upstairs – a cold anger smothered my own personal fears.

'In the name of Christ, and with all his mighty authority, I command you to leave that boy.'

The immediate response was a guttural scream, and the boy flung off his theatrical garb and ran into a bedroom. His mother and I climbed upwards to the landing. As we peered into a bedroom bathed in a green-reddish glow, the mother gasped. I automatically assumed that the lad had the fairly common disco lighting, but later discovered just an ordinary light bulb hanging from the ceiling.

Once again I repeated the command into the empty glow. There was still no sign of the boy. With the third repeat, the heavy divan bed left the floor and hit the ceiling, the impact being drowned by an inhuman roar as the boy emerged from underneath it and flew at his mother. He went for her neck, strangling with long bony fingers and bending her backwards over the landing banister. I wrestled to prise him loose. He eventually flung both of us aside, whirled into a second bedroom and almost wrenched the door from its hinges. The tussle which followed probably lasted for no more than a few minutes, but it seemed endless. Eventually the boy's eyes began to clear, the snarling was replaced by a frightened whimper and a shy, embarrassed fourteen-year-old emerged. The only thing which now seemed to disturb him was the vision of a large vicar sat on his chest! He had no recollection of the four-hour reign of terror he had just inflicted on his family.

After three months of counselling and help, the boy verbally invited Christ's Spirit into his life, and the following day he disappeared from view! Only later did we discover that, once free of evil visions and dreams, he wanted nothing more to do with spiritual things.

'I just want to be left alone to live a normal life with my mates,' he said. Sadly, it appeared to make little impression when I reminded him of Jesus' warnings about returning evil spirits, a topic we had previously discussed at length (Matthew 12:43f).

★   ★   ★

This kind of satanism is one extreme of the occult. We now move on to the large overlap area between the occult and paganism – witchcraft.

A broad-backed brooding hill dominates the landscape in the folds of the North-east Lancashire moors. Pendle, with its heritage of witchcraft, is a powerful magnet for occultists. The same is true for a hundred similarly rural scenes dotted about our increasingly pagan isles.

'We're here,' said one Pendle witch, 'because the power is here. This is our capital, our temple, and you Christians have no right to come and desecrate our holy place.'

The local churches at the time were trying to rally support

to erect a twenty foot high rolled-steel cross on the shoulder of a hill which had been a cradle of northern Christianity. Among other distinctions, Pendle had been the place where George Fox had his 'inner light' vision before starting the Quaker movement in the Puritan England of the 1640s.

The witch who had given me the warning about the cross – a barrel-chested dwarf balancing in his elevated boots – stood at the time on the pathway of my vicarage and looked up at me in defiance. He played nervously with his assorted occult jewellery and then pronounced a curse on our home and work. Several months later he was dead.[1] He had suffered a fatal asthmatic attack aboard a plane en route to an international magic convention in Mexico. As I read the details in the local evening paper, I felt tears sting the back of my eyes. Despite the dwarf's warnings and curses, I had taken a liking to him and had been looking forward to having a further chat at some later date. Now, there would be no more theological tussles, no chance to share with him how a dynamic relationship with Jesus could give him real power for living; no more opportunity to contrast true Christianity with the dreary deadness of the 'Churchianity' which had been inflicted upon him as a child.

*   *   *

Witchcraft had a membership explosion in the fifties and sixties after being legalised. This gave the impetus for the restoration of a far older form of the occult which has, in recent years, outstripped the more ritualised paganism known as *wicca*. This was magic!

This is not, I hasten to explain, the Paul Daniels type of television magic. Sleight of hand and clever illusion are rarely connected with the magic of that paganism which stretches beyond the alchemy of Merlin into the mists of prehistory.

I sat opposite an occult magician in a Blackpool pub. He

had refused to let me come to his home because his previous experience of Christians had fostered total distrust of them. We had spent an hour sparring verbally over our drinks when he eventually opened up.

'We can summon up whatever we need for our magic.' His voice had a take-it-or-leave-it tone and was tinged with the patience one uses when speaking to the uninitiated. 'If we need a six-foot rabbit, then that is what we summon up. If a demon is needed, then that will be produced.'

Had this come earlier in our conversation, the temptation would have been to dismiss both the statement and the mind which produced it. But in the previous hour, the man's intellect had been impressive. His grasp of the classical threads of philosophy was firm and comprehensive even though his understanding of reality was a chasm away from mine. He was a product of a dozen generations of Western thought which had struggled to construct a coherent atheism, but which rarely emerged above the clouds of agnosticism.

My heart went out to this man of intellect. Had I indicated as much, he would have shredded my patronising attitude with the sharp edge of his scorn. Instead, I spoke of an almighty personal force beyond ourselves, while he was more inclined to plumb the depths of his psyche in search of hidden power. For this magician, the effects of his rituals – the six-foot rabbit or the demon, for example – were nothing more than artificial creations manufactured from a power within the subconsciousness of himself and the rest of his magic circle.

*   *   *

We next come to the strangest of overlaps which incorporates Christianity with paganism and the occult.

'I'm a born-again Christian,' the professional clairvoyant announced as we sat in her studio during an unusually quiet slot between appointments. 'At one time I was heading for the mission field, but I believe God called me here instead.'

This is the fuzzy edge between the 'soft' occult and Christianity, where an alleged relationship with, or belief in, Christ often exists alongside the psychic phenomena. Straddling this line are a motley group who view Christ as either one of the greatest mediums who ever practised, or the Son of God whose psychic powers were honed to perfection. To these people personal experience is paramount, and certainly superior to the authority of Scripture. This is sadly true in some areas of the established Church. The Churches' Fellowship for Psychical and Spiritual Studies, based in Bromley, Kent, is one of the leaders in this twilight zone.

'We in the Churches' Fellowship,' writes the Chairman, the Venerable Michael Perry, Archdeacon of Durham, 'may not be up to the theological acrobatics of the professionals, but we must hold to the sanctity of our experience. When we are quizzed as to the value of the psychical gifts of which we have evidence, we should not be sidetracked, but should come out with 'one thing I know – whereas I was blind, now I see.'[2]

Experience-based beliefs have one major fault. They are only as perfect as man's imperfect feelings will allow. Mr Perry chooses to elevate his own mind and experience above Scripture, and he is consequently able to entertain unbiblical beliefs such as reincarnation and the non–existence of hell. We deal with this more fully in Chapter 13.

The Bible-based Christian will have the greatest difficulty digesting this cocktail of liberal Christianity and the soft occult. He may possibly find it easier to love the external 'heathen in his blindness' than to feel sympathy for the 'insider' who dares to re-interpret or re-state the beloved faith. It is much easier to condemn those considered too close for comfort. And yet, our calling is to approach all with the love of Christ even, for example, the Jeanne Dixons of this shadowy world. Mrs Dixon, an American Roman Catholic, is perhaps the world's most famous seeress. Is she a true prophet of God or, as others claim, one of Satan's most successful psychic mediums? How can she accurately predict so many world-shaking events days or months before they happen, such as the assassination of President John F Kennedy? Is it right to condemn a lady who claims to attend mass every day and insists that she has most of her visions during prayers? And what of the late Doris Stokes? This British medium, who also believed her powers were God-given, filled massive halls and was compulsive television viewing for millions before her recent death. She claimed to help thousands come to terms with the 'other world'.

The questions are posed. Again, the answers must wait for later pages as we continue our exploration of a pagan-occult world, the boundaries of which increasingly encroach on our culture and lifestyle.

★   ★   ★

And then there is the New Age.

You are able to read this book only because the world was saved from destruction on August 16th and 17th, 1987, by hundreds of thousands of New Agers gathered at sacred sites across the globe. You may not have been aware that you were even in peril, but dedicated groups of New Agers assure us that it would have been the end had they not interceded by staging their world-wide 'Hum Day'.

At one of the sites, Glastonbury Tor, Somerset, hundreds of hippies gathered to greet the dawning of the 'Age of Aquarius' by holding hands and humming loudly through clenched teeth. The same thing was happening at dozens of other sacred sites across the world[3] 'building up vibrations . . . to create positive forces that will help the earth to grow stronger and prevent a catastrophe,' said organiser Rosalie Samet in England.

August 16, according to an ancient Aztec legend, was

forecast as the end of the world. It was also the day when the old Mayan and Aztec calendars converged. This was twinned with American Hopi Indian legends which predicted doom unless 144,000 sundancers performed on this day.

If all this seems a bit eccentric for you, some authors are telling us today that it is only a taste of things to come. The New Age has swept across America and into many other Western cultures and will, it is claimed, become a strong force in Britain during the next decade.

At first glance, the New Age movement is simply a reaction against an ultra-materialistic Western society in which gold outweighs the soul. The respectable face of what is called the 'Age of Aquarius' is in the search for the 'real self', or a deeper concern for our ecology. It is the quest for peace and goodwill, pursued by a worldwide network of like-minded organisations with goals of establishing 'unity in diversity' in a New World Order.

The less savoury side is in the use of the occult practices to reach the inner self, and a new-look paganism which elevates nature to the status of a god. The movement seeks to transport the gurus and philosophers of the East into Western culture, and tries to resurrect ancient ways and old religions. For some Christian writers, it is the New Age of Satanism, a viable umbrella structure which comes alarmingly near to the 'great apostasy' or 'falling away' as prophesied by Paul (2 Thessalonians 2:3). It has its new messiah, the Lord Maitreya, the Master of Wisdom, who is variously known as Jesus, Brahma, Krishna and Muhammad.[4]

World-famous actress Shirley MacLaine takes her readers on 'a voyage into the realm of the Mind and Spirit' in her bestselling book *Out on a Limb*. She highlights many of the dubious areas now being widely explored by fellow 'Aquarians'. There are the trance-channellers, out-of-the-body experiences, hypnotic regressions to previous lives, reincarnation, near-death experiences, yoga and meditation, and parapsychology.

The New Agers are into mind-expanding, mind-altering techniques in a massive 'self-help' movement. They are determined to know and become all that they are capable of being, and often that is nothing short of divine! Miss MacLaine quotes approvingly one of her 'gurus' as saying, 'The skeptics' view of higher knowledge of self is most limiting. Your dogmatic religions, for example, are most limiting for mankind because they demand unquestioned reverence of authority. YOU are God. YOU know you are divine. But you must continually remember your Divinity and, most important, *act* accordingly.'[5]

★   ★   ★

Paganism and the occult are also now finding a lucrative and growing market in the world of fantasy games. Some education authorities are becoming so alarmed that they have begun to vet books and computer games used in their schools. Leading publishers have been approached to tone down the violence and occult content, especially in children's books. One or two responded immediately to an approach by the Evangelical Alliance in 1986,[6] but the majority refused to listen. There is now evidence that fantasy-occult games may have been a contributing factor in the bloodiest one-man massacre in Britain's history.

In August, 1987, 32 people were killed or injured in the Berkshire village of Hungerford by Michael Ryan after he received a challenge to 'kill his fellow Terrans' in a mail-order fantasy game. Mr Paul Borreson, one of the two brothers who still run The Swindon War and Fantasy Games Club, told me that it was 'rubbish' to associate the game's challenge with the Hungerford massacre. He explained, 'Michael Ryan received his instructions a full six weeks before the killings.'

Mr Borreson said that Michael Ryan, at the time he received his instructions, was fifth in the game's league, and that he had to score more points by showing that he could kill the 'Terrans'.

'It was obvious who the Terrans were,' said Mr Borreson. 'They were his rivals in the game. There are a whole range of ways of killing, such as sword fights, duels or even casting magic spells.'

Mr Borreson said that they 'rested' the games for about two weeks after the Hungerford killings. During this time 'we made them even more normal, even more game-like,' he added. The company then resumed trading as normal.

Frank Thompson, a Daily Mail reporter, who 'scooped' the story, spoke to me of his suspicions when he first learned the facts. Only after he discounted the 'publicity-seeking' angle did he file his story.

'Mr Borreson and his brother were interviewed by the police twice,' he said, 'but they could not show the police positive proof that Ryan subscribed to the game. I was eventually satisfied that the brothers were genuine.' Thames Valley Police press office confirmed to me that this was one of their lines of inquiry. The official police report stated that Ryan 'was a man without friends who with his mother created a world of fantasy around which much of their life revolved'.

Ryan was known as Phodius Tei in the postal game called 'Further into Fantasy'. He played out the role of a high priest to a serpent god and was fearless and cruel. Ryan was sent the following instructions.

'When at last you awake, you are standing in a forest. There is a throbbing in your head, a madness . . . You know what to do, what power is to be gained from this.'

This arrived just six weeks before Ryan's murder rampage which began with the killing of a mother in Savernake forest. Another instruction for Phodius Tei reads, 'Rifle in hand ready to fire, you . . . begin to head down the stairs.'

In a shouted conversation from his top-floor refuge in a school, Ryan was asked by Police Sergeant Paul Brightwell if he knew how many he had shot.

'I don't know,' Ryan shouted back, 'it's like a bad dream.' Minutes later he shot himself.

$$\star \quad \star \quad \star$$

The brief tour of our subject is over. It is time to step with me into the detail. Here, the facts are far more heartbreaking, and the need for the light of Christ's love and compassion a hundredfold more evident. In accepting this invitation, beware of your motives. If you seek spiritual titillation, you may not be dissatisfied in the short-term, but equally you may find it harmful in your future Christian life. This book does not set out to provide vicarious thrills but to help each of us help those who are involved in a sad deception.

We need to understand the gods of the occult and the New Age of paganism before we can win any chance of a hearing. The first principle of communication is to understand the other person's position. Paul illustrated this perfectly when he spoke to the limited knowledge of his hearers in Athens. Beginning with their unknown god, he went on to sketch the features of the one true God.

The whole armour of God

To approach occultists with love is a dangerous and demanding business. It calls for spiritual discernment of the highest order, and only God's mighty and protective Holy Spirit can provide it. Christians need to recognise that these people live down their streets. Nine out of ten people in our nation believe in the reality of at least one aspect of the paranormal and the occult.[7] You may have never knowingly met a witch or a satanist, for they live in chosen anonymity on your estate. But you will have met their distant 'relatives'.

There is that next-door neighbour, for instance, who cannot seem to make a decision without consulting her horoscope. There is the aunt who is into seances because she yearns to contact her dead husband, or the friend who is keen on palm reading or tea-leaf divination. Paganism and the occult are down your street.

Before approaching those involved or affected, we need the protection of the whole armour of God (Ephesians 6:10f). Soldiers who go to war without training and weapons should not be surprised if they get shot! The soldier of Christ is constantly reminded in Scripture that he is a frontline trooper in spiritual warfare, and that the enemy can appear in more forms and terrains than the imagination can manage. Paul warns against being conformed to the patterns of the opposition (Romans 12:2), and yet the standards of this world can often be unconsciously absorbed. Modern thought patterns are intricately etched with the paranormal, psychical, neo-paganism and the occult, the absorption of which can be as lethal to the soul as germ warfare is to the body.

Before you accept this invitation to venture where angels really do fear to tread, get in touch with the Lord and ask for his guidance and help. Remind yourself that you are 'protected by the blood of Jesus' (1 John 5:18); that you are all-conquering through Christ (Romans 8:37), and that the devil must flee when you resist him (James 4:7). In fact, why not set aside this book right now, and take time to ensure that you are firmly grounded in the Lord's power and promises. The book can wait. . . .

2

The Resurrection of Paganism

There are numerous reasons for the resurrection of paganism, but first we need to review the devil's main strategy.

Divide and conquer

Confuse and cripple your enemy's communications and you can start to plan your victory celebrations. The strategy is as old as war. Gideon's small 'speed and shock' force, outnumbered more than four hundred to one, confused and then annihilated the Midianites with similiar tactics (Judges 7). Commanders in the last world war took a few leaves from Scripture when they set up the Special Operations Executive (SOE) and the Special Air Service (SAS). General Eisenhower credited SOE activities with shortening the war by almost a year.

'Give me one SOE agent,' he said, 'he is worth fifteen divisions!'

Naval Intelligence, knowing that Hitler and some of his immediate staff were dabblers in the occult, leaked the rumour that the pendulum-swinging method was Britain's secret weapon in their increased success in locating and destroying the underwater enemy. Actually, scientific research had revealed that U-boats were able to dive below 600 feet, previously thought to have been an impossibility, and that, consequently, allied depth charges had been wasted because of wrong settings. Within days of the false leak, the Germans had diverted some of their best brains to form a Pendulum Intelligence Team under Captain Hans Roeder. It was months before the truth of this little trick dawned and by that time the U-boat war had begun to swing in England's favour.[1]

In the spiritual warfare of the last 2,000 years, a devious enemy has employed this strategy to subvert communications between the various divisions of Christ's army, and between them and the Divine General.

Paganism once had a monopoly in 'England's green and pleasant land' and nobody knows for sure whose were the first Christian feet to 'walk upon our mountains green'.[2] The first threat to the dark, satanic 'hills' of England was probably in the form of converted merchants and soldiers. They brought a dynamic 'Acts of the Apostles' Christianity to our shores, though there is some evidence that the apostle Paul might have beaten them to it.[3] There were certainly native bishops by 314AD but the satanic 'principalities and powers' overseeing our sceptred isles at that time were probably not unduly alarmed by what must have only amounted to irritating 'guerrilla' activities. Christian influence was certainly confined to remote Celtic churches and exercised little influence. The real invasion did not come for another three hundred years, with the help of a lady with the unlikely name of Bertha. She was a Christian princess of the Franks, who had caught the eye of the King of Kent, Ethelbert. He also happened to be the leading force among the Anglo-Saxons south of the Humber. Meanwhile, Rome decided it was ripe to have its man in England, and the reluctant Augustine was despatched. The devil's forces now had a real battle on their hands, for within a handful of years Ethelbert had been baptised, and Canterbury had its first Archbishop. At the same time, the invincible partnership of

Aidan, from Iona, and Oswald, the recently converted King of Northumbia, was 'attacking' from the north.

Rome to the south and a rejuvenated Celtic church to the north caught the devil's paganism in a pincer movement. What now was to be his strategy?

A seaside place called Whitby was probably his answer, plus a tiff in the royal bedchamber! Celtic King Oswy, Oswald's successor on the Northumbrian throne, discovered that he would be celebrating Easter while his southern wife, influenced by Rome, would still be in the ashes of Lent. Historians tell us that King Oswy chaired the Synod of Whitby which was called to decide the date of Easter, once and for all. The King not only had to contend with his wife but also the Pope of the day. Should he follow local Celtic custom and keep a few Ionan monks happy, or should he bow to the 'keeper of heaven's gates' in Rome and the continued favour of his wife? Historians suggest that there was no real contest.

Whatever the reason, England joined mainstream continental Christianity, and was to be subsequently caught up in centuries of political and theological wranglings. Ironically, Whitby was to feature in more modern times in the renaissance of the occult.

The devil's trap had been sprung. A living, Bible-based Celtic church, left to grow and develop, would have brought a speedy end to paganism. God's powerful Spirit might have swept the native religion into folklore, as he did in many countries in later church history. But for England, set firmly under the domination of man and his growing traditions – which often contradicted scriptural Christianity – the debilitating struggle was to grind on wearily. Paganism was to exist alongside, and mixed up with, Christianity until well beyond the Middle Ages when it was eventually outlawed. This was only achieved through a massive reformation of the Church and the restoration of God's foundational authority – the Bible.

The devil's next tactic was to convince the increasingly educated masses and the church in general that their link with God through Scripture was unreliable. This was all but achieved by the late nineteenth century. The devil might have masterminded the strategy but it was left to the 'world and the flesh' to add the finishing touches. History teaches one great truth: man can inflict far more damage on himself than even the devil on occasions. If the devil were annihilated today, men and women could still keep evil alive. The devil encouraged man to deify his own brain during the Age of Enlightenment, and in an Age of Romance besotted man fell in love with the beauty of creation while increasingly ignoring the Creator.

Man was consequently cast adrift in a sea of conflicting philosophical currents without compass, charts, or indeed any secure knowledge that there was in fact any place to go. No longer could he know truth, he was told, nor even that such a thing as truth existed. He could only find what was true for himself while others, heading in the opposite direction, would have to find 'their own truth'. In his lost new world, tolerance became man's greatest virtue . . . the perfect environment for the devil to lead anybody up his garden path. He could even convince modern, mixed-up man that he himself did not exist but was merely a music hall joke with a pair of horns and a barbed tail – about as real as any comic book monster.[4] Certainly, it was the ideal time to re-instate the old ways of paganism, and in 1951 parliament had to oblige, following the acceptance of the United Nations Charter which granted freedom of worship to all. There was also the disastrous 'Crown versus Helen Duncan' case when a bogus medium was inappropriately tried under the old Witchcraft Act. Modern man reasoned that nobody could tell others how to worship because now there was no one true way or God. In any case, it was suggested, the legalising of witchcraft would have no affect on a sophisticated nation nor its people. . . .

Within 15 years, according to many of my contacts within the occult, witchcraft membership had multiplied at least a hundred fold! It is conservatively estimated that there are now more than 30,000 practising witches in Britain.

Witchcraft takes off

Throughout the fifties and early sixties, books on witchcraft, satanism and the occult in general, by writers such as Gerald Gardner and Aleister Crowley, flooded a now legitimate market. Much of their thinking was popularised by Dennis Wheatley. As a committed Roman Catholic, this might not have been his intention, and indeed he alwas ensured that good triumphed in his final chapters. However his best-selling books certainly introduced me to the occult in my youth. A clairvoyant of my age, who was experiencing psychic disturbances, was counselled by her minister and warned against the 'evils of the devil'. The minister then gave her a copy of Wheatley's *The Devil Rides Out* to show her how evil the devil really was.

'I took one look at it,' the girl later told me, 'and I was hooked. I couldn't put it down until I had reached the end. From then on, I knew where I was going – and it wasn't towards Christianity.'

These writers then, were the pathfinders for what is now a multi-million dollar media industry. In the last thirty years the number of covens has grown to rival the churches in some areas, and around my corner of the world there are as many witches as there are church leaders. The number of occult bookshops in our towns and cities has not yet equalled the Christian equivalents but may well exceed them within the next decade.

As chapels and churches close there have been attempts to purchase at least one for use as a temple of witchcraft.[5] Some occultists sense a certain victory in taking over that which was previously Christian, or repossessing an old pagan site on which a church has been built. Sometimes, as in the case of one beautiful and historical church (circa 1090 AD), occultists prefer to purchase an old church simply because its architecture makes it eminently suitable for the practice of group ritual.

Enter chaos

Witchcraft – paganism in its purest form – is one of the oldest of religions, and as such has collected together a creed of doctrines. In our 'anything goes' culture, the majority entering the occult found this too limiting. They wanted freedom from the morals and dogmas of the wicca religion[6] (see Chapter 7), and the growing tensions eventually exploded in 1980 during an occult convention – at Whitby!

A seed-idea for a new path of magic was conceived, though its germination and growth had to wait for a later symposium at East Morton, near Leeds. This yielded the latest occult craze – Chaos Magic. Additional nourishment was applied to this fast-growing off-shoot with the backing of 'The Sorcerer's Apprentice', an international occult mail order firm in Leeds.

The fall of Christianity and its biblical authority, plus the adoption of an 'anything goes' permissiveness, is the main reason for the resurrection of paganism. The devil, however, has a few more tactics which need to be considered.

More availability

Gone now is the traditional mystery and secrecy which for centuries has encircled the occult arts. You can now have your own home study course in occultism at a package deal price of £99.75, and if you really want to achieve mastery of the occult you can add to it the Complete Temple Course for a discount price of £235.99 (normally £247.64).[7] One major reason for the increased interest in the occult is that salesmanship and efficient business methods have stepped into the field. Not only are these occultists professional, but for the most part, they seem to have a genuine belief in what they are selling. Evangelism in the high street is now part of the occult.

More time

Voluntary and enforced leisure time is a modern curse to many – not surprising since man was designed to work six days a week (Exodus 20:9–10) rather than the modern four or five days. Boredom haunts many today, and some find an escape through the occult. Even the unemployed can join in, and many do. Various paths are open to the magician on the dole, and he is urged to, for instance, convert an old bread knife rather than purchase an expensive symbolically-adorned Solomonic sword for a Qabbalistic rite.[8]

There is ample evidence that an old, well-known adage still holds true: The devil is still finding work for idle hands!

More power

This is the primary goal of the occult. Power over employment, power for improving love prospects, altering adverse circumstances, engineering a more dominant personality, influencing friends, relatives, and even enemies, and exercising control over difficult environments. The occult vocabulary stresses mastery magnetism, domination, potency, authority, prestige, ascendancy and manipulation.

It coincides with that which supremely interested Lucifer. There are hints in Scripture that his downfall came because he craved to be the most powerful being in the universe, and only God stood in his way (Revelation 12:9; Luke 10:18; Ezekiel 28 and Isaiah 14). There are a few megalomaniacs today who desire universal power, but many more who would love to have influence over people and things surrounding them. Millions of little men yearn to be gods in their own tiny castles, and the occult is only too happy to help.

Simon, the sorcerer, in the Book of Acts, had the same desire. When Simon saw that the Spirit was given at the laying on of the Apostles' hands, he offered them money and said, 'Give me also this ability so that everyone on whom I lay hands may receive the Holy Spirit! (8:18, 19) Simon realised that for all the mighty wonders he had performed, he was still a long way short of the supreme power which only God could give. He had had the crowds enthralled by his magic, so amazed that they called him 'the Great Power'. That was until Philip, Peter and John came along with God's greater power. Peter cursed Simon's money and told him that a 'right heart' was the only appropriate currency to gain God's almighty power.

Today occult magicians sadly do not know what real power is. They play with what amount to destructive toys because they refuse to grow up into the real men God designed them to be.

More knowledge

There are gossips who just cannot wait to tell you what you do not know. There are the world's 'know-alls' who delight to show you how much more they know than you do. And then there are the infuriating 'modern gnostics', the ones who smile down at you from the heights to which their superior knowledge has elevated them. Last of all there are the 'Eves' of this world who have found something deliciously naughty and cannot wait until you too have been enticed. You find them at every party offering 'goodies' in the form of drugs, drink, sex and the occult.

People delight in the one-up-manship which extra know-ledge affords them, and the occult is always ready to seduce in this direction. There is the spurious promise of knowledge about the dear departed through mediums, or details of past lives courtesy of the dubious skills of regression hypnotists. Exciting tit-bits from the future are on offer via crystal balls, tarot cards, palmistry and astrology.

It is the original lure of Satan and one of his most subtle and effective temptations. Eve was bewitched by it.

'You will not surely die,' the serpent said to the woman. 'For God knows that when you eat of it your eyes will be opened, and you will be like God, knowing good and evil' (Genesis 3:4,5).

This is the knowledge that destroys, or deceives and invariably disappoints. The devil is not in business to provide his disciples with truth, in fact 'the god of this age' is much more interested in blinding 'the minds of unbelievers, so that they cannot see the light of the gospel of the glory of Christ, who is the image of God' (2 Corinthians 4:4).

More life

'Come on, Joanne, let's have a bit of fun!'

It was an offer that schoolgirl Joanne could not refuse.

'Anything to break the monotony,' she thought. Life was as boring as an algebraic equation; as depressing as a two-hour homework stint; as purposeless as those boring RE lessons at school.

The fun offered was to be another 'fix' for a teenager addicted to the future. The best antidote Joanne had found to those stale days was a bewitching gaze into what tomorrow held. The fun promised by Joanne's friend was a lesson on how to tell her own future at the turn of the occult picture cards. She had reached for the stars but wanted more. As time went by, even the tarot cards did not bring complete satisfaction, so she next tried for a penpal by advertising in a monthly occult magazine.

Joanne's story so far is typical of many of today's schoolchildren. In a recent survey of nearly 300 fourth-formers in two Lancashire schools, we found that 87% had dabbled in the occult (44% of them with ouija boards). The survey, conducted under teacher supervision, also revealed that 13% found the occult helpful, 20% watched occult films or videos monthly or even weekly, and that for more than 5% the occult was a regular part of their lifestyle. If this last figure is an accurate pointer for the rest of the nation's secondary schools, we are facing an appalling occult boom in the rising generation.

The Evangelical Alliance (EA) produced a disturbing fact-sheet showing that Dan Dare and Biggles are being superseded by excursions into the twilight world of the occult.[9] One 'fun book' included a chant to call up the devil spirit and, on a more subtle front, the EA found 'books that included overtones of incest; assorted black magic; a story where a little girl arranged for a ghost to mutilate her baby brother; clairvoyance used as a good force; and children putting ghosts to rest'. Fantasy books, in which readers contribute to the plots by deciding what happens next, take children into an imaginary world of evil and occult intrigue. One book, aimed at nine to twelve year olds, carries a spine-chilling description of an equivalent to a black mass, says the EA leaflet.

> Hundreds of black-cowled figures kneel at prayer in the dark-vaulted church . . . a golden chalice is being passed . . . blood drips from his vampire fangs. He hands you the chalice and you have to drink. It is human blood, cursed in death's name. It curdles in your stomach, and you are seized by a palsy. . . .[10]

The leaflet explains that psychologists and social workers are already having to deal with the impact of fantasy books and computer games. Assessing the danger, one senior consultant psychiatrist said, 'I have seen a number of adult patients who have suffered psychological damage as a result of exposure to this kind of material. I am therefore very strongly opposed to the presentation of such material for children.'

The EA told me some months after the realease of the leaflet that several education authorities were acting upon it, and one publisher had withdrawn the book which included the chant to call up the devil spirit. Other publishers had been reluctant to discuss the leaflet's findings and were not inclined to act on the matter.

'Publishers,' stated the EA, 'either through ignorance or greed, are prepared to exploit our childrens' emotions and experience – putting minds and imaginations at risk.'

More spiritual life

'The vast majority of satanists,' one occult magician told me, 'are ex-Roman Catholics or from the high Anglo–Catholics.' A witch, who was also an honours–degree theological student at Manchester University, said that it was similar in witchcraft.

'They had all tried the church, but you had nothing to offer them,' the occult magician added.

Similiar comments from others in the occult indicate that the church of the last generation has a lot for which it has to answer. It seems that if spiritual man cannot find satisfaction in the churches, he is prepared to look elsewhere, even in the reverse of Christianity.

In our schools' survey, nearly half those questioned believed that man had a spiritual side to his nature, more than one in three were not too sure. But only 16% gave a definite 'no'. Over half found the church boring or a waste of time, and one in three said they had no opinion because they had never been to church.

It would seem that the church must bear some of the responsibility for the rise in occultism. Those who had entered after an upbringing in, or experience of, dead 'churchianity' found it difficult to accept that there was anything more to Christianity than what they had already seen. They had been innoculated against the real and infect-ious vibrancy of true Christianity!

One witch told me, 'Your Christianity cannot offer me the supernatural. Why, many of you don't even believe in miracles. We have them as almost weekly occurrences!' He gave the impression of overstating his point, but only slightly.

If you think this is being a little hard on the church, come with me back to Acts 8 once again. The people of Samaria took one look at what Philip had to offer and promptly gave sorcerer Simon the thumbs-down. There was just no comparison between the power of the Holy Spirit and the counterfeit magic of the occult. Many of today's church leaders and theologians have ruled out a God who wants to break into lives and history. They do not even accept that he did it two thousand years ago, and are determined to erase any hint of the miraculous from Scripture. They offer only a thin leaflet of nice thoughts and a flimsy, gossamer gospel.

Thank God that in an increasing number of individual churches the Holy Spirit is seen to be alive and well and still pouring abundant, supernatural life into his true followers.

More media interest

The media have popularised the occult and the paranormal through films like *Rosemary's Baby*, *The Exorcist* and *Poltergeist*. The press have also helped. In the week of typing this chapter, the Sunday Express gave a half-page story – almost a free advertisement – to one mail order occult firm, and a two-page spread to a facet of witchcraft in its colour supplement.[11] Both received sympathetic treatment.

Industry has also cashed in on the boom. As this book goes to press six famous companies are using psychic, para-normal or occult (features) in their television commercials. An empty toffee wrapper floats down during a seance; a twinkling, slightly-roguish devil promotes cream cakes or a temptingly rich chocolate bar, and an international footwear firm wins the kids over to wearing its magic shoes with the aid of a friendly witch. A famous brewery has invested £5 million to make its product attractive to the nature-loving, individualist breed of the New-Age 1990s drinker. Its television commercials have a Celtic, elemental flavour with a central character who arrives from outer space. He appeals to the individualist, and yet entices the drinker to be one of his crowd. He is the personification, the 'alter ego' of the drink, dressed all in black and topped with a foam of blond hair. If Guinness were a man, this is what he would look like![12]

Modern psychological advertising tries to reach us by playing on our innermost images and emotions. The subjects of this book are particularly helpful in reaching at least two categories. There is the reformer who is interested in the quality of life, its meaning, its naturalness. This person is often a professional who is out to influence society and change its foundational beliefs. The second category are the succeeders. These are the people who have arrived, or who are on their way; the people who like power and feel ill at ease if they are not in control. A third group are the mainstream consumers, those who want security and always go for the well-known brands. This group, however, love a little mystery, perhaps a hint of Black Magic, so long as it does not seem too much of a risk. An impish, non-threatening devil is tailor-made for this market.

One national store launched a new outlet with centre-spread advertisements promising, through the crystal ball, a future in which shoppers' palms would be crossed with silver, because of bargain savings. The tarot cards predicted an easy time ahead for shoppers and the store's name was spelt out in the tea-leaves.[13] ASDA price comes courtesy of occult advertising, not because the firm is that way inclined, but because they know that Mr and Mrs Average Shopper is! After all, the firm, and other national companies, are not likely to spend millions on advertising which does not speak to the interests of those they are trying to reach.

Market research tells them that 90% of people give some credence to the supernatural and paranormal. They know that the power which made five hundred Yorkshire house-wives lose £10,000 from their husbands' collective wage packets on the word of a fortune-teller, is just as likely to sell their products. The wages were forfeited when a pitman's wife received a poor reading in the crystal ball, and urged her husband not to go down the mine on a certain day. The warning travelled on the mining community's efficient grapevine and five hundred miners stayed at home.

*   *   *

Other reasons for the rise in occultism include a disenchant-ment with several generations of materialism, a turning back to the old ways of nature; a hunger for thrills and pleasure; a yearning for the secrecy and comradeship of an exclusive group; or merely a fascination with the bizarre.

3

To the Occult with Reason

Many modern churchmen dismiss such things as demons, devils, and possession as psychological disorders. In 1974 sixty-five Anglican theologians in an open letter to the 'Daily Telegraph' stated that it was dangerous to encourage the belief that there were occult evil powers which could possess people. This was in response to a much-publicised exorcism which went tragically wrong. Lurid stories under tabloid headlines proclaimed that a man had returned home after an exorcism and gouged out his wife's eyes, killing her.

Occultists of the eighties would explain that devils and demons were merely artificial manifestations which the mind can induce when it is disengaged from normal rationality. They often deliberately use the rituals of magic to create an altered state of consciousness when reason is suspended. They insist that in doing so, they are manipulating a neutral magical force within themselves. They join with derisive modern churchmen in maintaining that it is naive to take the devil as a literal personal force for evil.

As for the ordinary man in the street, he will publicly laugh off demon phenomena as the products of over-zealous imaginations, or dismiss them as the fiction of frauds. But in private, and for opinion polsters, the vast majority will admit some form of belief in the supernatural.

Not all churchmen dismiss the real existence of demons and the devil, by any means. In fact, the General Synod of the Church of England set up a working party to apply biblically-directed reason to the problem. The Bishop of Exeter's Report on Exorcism, complete with sensible guidelines, was the eventual result.[1] Let us also apply similar reason to a trio of commonly-asked questions concerning the occult . . .

Is there really a devil?

Too many unanswered questions remain if we dismiss the devil as a myth; a character invented to personify evil and to help the simple folk of yesteryear visualise the power of their own temptations. Take a look at some of the problems we meet.

I look at the world.

We are crippling our planet with pollution. The white man is en route to an horrendous bloodbath because he insists on treating the black man as less than himself. We spend the world's resources as though there will be no tomorrow, despite being constantly reminded that, if we keep on at the present rate, there will be nothing left. There is already a hole half the size of Europe in the earth's protective ozone layer. Why does sophisticated, educated, modern man not apply the brakes on his mad helter-skelter to destruction? Just what is it that produces such inertia and blindness? Could it be that man is not in control and that an external destructive power is?

I look to reason.

Reason and experience tell me that everything in this world has an opposite. Christian writer Michael Green asks, 'If a Holy Spirit, why not an unholy spirit?'[2] Socrates said on his death bed that he believed in the existence of an evil spirit which meant that there must be a good spirit.

If a person dabbles in Christianity by going to church, he can end up being possessed by the Holy Spirit. Of course, God is a gentleman and will never force himself on anybody. The 'dabbling' has to be accompanied by repentanc and a determination to accept Jesus Christ as Lord. The devil does not, however, accept the same ground rules. If a person dabbles in the occult at any level, he need not be surprised to find himself playing host to some dubious spirit.

The law of cause and effect needs also to be considered. Man has yet to discover an 'effect' which has not been caused by something else. The atheist claims the universe has no cause, but the nearer he moves to the brink of our beginnings, the more agnostic he becomes. He may claim that our universe resulted from the 'Big Bang'. But what caused a lump of dense matter, supposedly no bigger than a sack of potatoes, to explode? The atheist resorts to the laws of physics. But where did these laws come from? This is generally the point at which logic forces the atheist to convert to agnosticism.

Everything in our world appears to have a cause, and so it is not unreasonable to assume the world itself has a cause. We have given that First Cause a name – God.

Chapter 15 shows that it is eminently reasonable to accept Scripture as a further revelation from this God. We learn in this book that he gave men and angels freedom to choose good or evil. It is also reasonable to accept the biblical explanation of the devil, the chief angel who chose to defect, and is now bent on dragging the rest of God's creation into his revolution (Genesis 3; Isaiah 14:12–20; 2 Corinthians 4:3f).

I look at the Church.

The first duty of Christians is to worship God, but we are too busy idolising our separate traditions.

Jesus, for instance, gave the Lord's Table of unity. In our

hands it disintegrates into splinters! The act of remembrance designed to bring closer communion with God and each other becomes a spiritual Iron Curtain! Meanwhile some raise their hands in praise while others throw them up in horror!

Since 1910 the denominations have fought for unity – and we are still fighting today! Why do we appear to have no control? Is something or somebody else pulling the strings and keeping us apart?

Our second commission is to evangelise or witness, but for centuries we have left it to the professional with the 'dog-collar'. The church dies because the 'manufacture' of new Christians is left to the church leader. Industry would collapse overnight if the managing director was the only production worker. Commerce would be a shambles if all the office staff spent their time running raffles, socials and jumble sales while the office manager did the typing. The survival of Christianity in Western Europe, considering its selfish, suicidal membership, is a constant miraculous monument to an all-powerful, intervening God. It also provides supportive evidence that somebody is trying to shut the gates against every directive that God ever gave his work force. Jesus tells us that those gates belong to hell (Matthew 16:18).

I look at the family.

Most social commentators warn that the basic building block of society is crumbling. The cement of godliness is cracked and the binding agent of morality has lost its grip. One in five babies is born out of wedlock, 400 abortions are carried out each day in England and Wales, and the divorce rate has more than doubled in the last fifteen years. Half the marriages involving a partner under thirty five end on the rocks. The number of first-time marriages has dropped alarmingly, revealing that more and more prefer to co-habit without, life-long, legally binding commitments.[3]

Men and women are increasingly controlled by a 'throw-away' mentality. Unborn babies are tossed into incinerators, marriage promises are cast aside, and home life is consigned to the scrap heap. And yet no husband or wife deliberately seeks heartbreak and tragedy. Often the choice seems to be taken out of their hands by the 'spirit of the age'.

It becomes increasingly evident who that 'spirit' is as we look at the remaining areas.

I look into the occult.

The modern magician is pragmatic. He is not particularly interested in morality, ethics, or goodness. He wants something that works. If it does not work, then he is not interested. The results must be evident. And so they are! When he launches himself into what he calls 'the void', he knows that without adequate controls he can be destroyed by the external powers he meets. Occult home-study books and tapes constantly emphasise this danger to the beginner. Consider also the schoolboy at the beginning of my first chapter, and thousands of others like him, who become demonized. Nobody who has seen this happen, or experienced it themselves, can ever doubt the existence of a personal, evil power. It is an education to be wrestling with a frenzied demoniac one moment, and the next to be calmly reassuring a timid teenager who wonders what on earth has been happening to him.

The resurgence of interest in the paranormal, the psychic, magic and paganism has persuaded many that the spirit realm and the devil are a reality.

I look into the Bible.

We might be forgiven for turning the devil into a joke if he and his forces were only casually mentioned in some obscure poetic book. The fact is that it is hard to find a page on which the devil or evil do not feature, either implicitly or explicitly. From Adam to the last Amen, Satan is the 'falling-star' of

Scripture, and almost every writer is inspired to speak against his abode, his effects, his activities and his purposes.

I look at Jesus.

Satan was no myth to the Son of God. It would be difficult to dismiss as a figment of your imagination a devil who lifts you to the roof of the Temple, or whisks you high on to a mountain top (Matthew 4). Jesus's main mission was to destroy the works of the evil one (1 John 3:8), and to drive out the prince of this world by his victorious death on Calvary (John 12: 31,32). He even taught his disciples to ask for deliverance from the evil one (Matthew 6:13), gave them authority to cast out demons (Matthew 10:1), and spoke of the time he saw Satan fall from heaven (Luke 10:17f). Jesus took the devil seriously, and this seems a stronger argument than even the collected words and works of all the modernist theologians and materialists.

I look into myself.

I know what I should be. I identify each of my failings and yearn to be better. I cry out with Paul, the apostle, 'I do not understand what I do. For what I want to do I do not do, but what I hate I do' (Romans 7:15). Nero's tutor Seneca said, 'All of my life I have been seeking to climb out of the pit of my besetting sins, and I cannot do it; and I never will unless a hand is let down to draw me up.' Mark Twain wrote, 'Man is the only animal that blushes – or needs to!' Tennyson yearned for a better Tennyson in his poetry,

> Ah for a man to arise in me
> That the man I am, may cease to be.

Resolutions are made and unmade often in the same day. Temptation is cunning and clever, devious and deceitful, and I seem to have no internal power to overcome a power from without. I admit that my 'will power is the matchstick under the uneven table–leg of life'.[4] I wobble, and even when I seem stabilised, it takes only a nudge to set me off again. I have to reach for Christ's power, and after allowing him to conquer one fault, I have to be constantly on guard lest I am tempted and fall in another direction. The Bible makes clear the identity of the tempter.

What about demons and evil spirits?

Consider: you are mighty but not almighty . . . you do not possess the attribute of being in all places at once . . . you do not have all knowledge . . . but you do have a rather large enterprise to run. Your only solution is to employ the services of others, structure your company under delegated powers and assume the position of chairman of the board.

Translate this into a universal consortium, and you have a reasonable analogy of the devil's position. He may well have been Lucifer, the brightest object of God's creation (as implied in Luke 10:18 and Revelation 9:1 and 12:9), but he has his limitations. He is called 'Beelzebub', the prince of demons (Matthew 12:24f; Mark 3:20f), and it would be appropriate to regard demons as his subjects or agents. A hierarchy of demons is implied in the descriptions of 'rulers . . . authorities . . . powers of this dark world . . . spiritual forces (agents) of evil in the heavenly realms' (Ephesians 6:12). There is the implication that evil spirits are delegated to oversee cities and nations, to delay or prevent the Lord's work being done in them (Daniel 10:12f).

I suspect that I am being far too complimentary in my description of hell's demons. Organisation and efficiency are not their strongest attributes. To understand this, we need to consider their origins.

There are many references in the Bible to the fall of Satan and the angels who sided with him (Revelation 12:9; Job 4:18b; Matthew 25:41; 2 Peter 2:4). There are implications that a third of the angels were swept out of heaven along with the devil (Revelation 12:4,9; Daniel 8:10). We have to be careful not to take the poetic sections in Scripture too literally, but Bible scholars over the centuries have deemed it safe to state that, at the very least, there was a heavenly war in which the losing minority were punished with exile. We can further assume, with safety, that those in opposition to God were not the most selfless of beings. We would still not be exaggerating to say that they were out to grab power, to seize control, to steal what was not theirs. They are still selfish, undisciplined, disobedient, liars, thieves, rebels and generally the last recruits you would dream of enlisting.

But the devil had no choice. In earthly terms, his self-centred mercenaries must have proved quite a headache over the centuries. There is also an innate stupidity in hell, which probably comes from not knowing the truth. New Zealand preacher Winkie Pratney calls it the 'whoops' factor. Demons and spirits affecting people, he said, often went too far and showed their presence and intent by some silly mistake.

None of the above should, however, lull us into a false sense of security. The devil is powerful, so are his forces, and even God's beings treat him with a certain measured respect (Jude 9). So should we. One might almost feel sympathy for Satan's plight but for the damage he and his forces do.

The work of demons – they are also called evil, bad, familiar,[5] lying and elemental[6] spirits – can be so damaging that Christians are urged to test for deceiving spirits (1 Corinthians 12:2,3; 1 Timothy 4:1). The difference between a good spirit and a bad spirit is always the same as the difference between a believer and a non-believer. The good spirit will be in an obedient relationship with God, he will never curse Jesus and all he stands for, but will acknowledge him as Lord (1 Corinthians 12:3). The bad spirit is unable to acknowledge the lordship of Christ but, in his deceiving ways, he will often fall just short of this point as he attempts to portray an acceptable face. Peter thought he was on the right lines when he offered to defend Jesus against all comers. He was amazed when Jesus turned on him and said,

'Get behind me, Satan! You are a stumbling block to me; you do not have in mind the things of God, but the things of men' (Matthew 16:23).

At least some demons have personalities and a high degree of intelligence. Many recognised Jesus and declared him to be the Son of God (Mark 3:11f). They communicated with each other (Matthew 12:43f), and they shudder because of God (James 2:19). On one occasion an evil spirit even discerned that the seven sons of Sceva (Acts 19:13f) were false exorcists and attacked them.

'Jesus I know, and I know about Paul,' said the evil spirit, 'but who are you?' The sons were given such a severe beating that they ran away naked and bleeding.

Demons can invade and possess (Matthew 17:18), deceive (2 Corinthians 4:4), injure and attempt murder (Mark 9:25–27), perform miracles and incite to war (Revelation 16:14), cause dumbness, epilepsy, blindness and deformity (Matthew 9:32; 17:15; 12:22). One of their chief aims is to lead people away from the faith (1 Timothy 4:1).

What does it mean to be possessed?

We have inherited this word from the Authorised Version of the Bible. Later versions have also struggled using phrases or words such as 'people with demons' (Good News), 'demoniacs' (RSV), and 'demon-possessed' (NIV). The original Greek means 'to be as a demon' or 'to be demon-ised', neither of which means a great deal to the average Englishman. The latter, even though it is the most accurate, reminds me of a do-it-yourself car-waxing product! Of course, we cannot help but struggle as we try to describe the indescribable. Possession by demons means all sorts to all people depending on which books, films, and horror-stories they have experienced. Only those who have been affected

by demons, and possibly those who minister in this area, can
know the full meaning of the word.

Many ministering in the occult dislike using the word
'possession' because it does not truly reflect the whole range
of states which are encountered. There are, for instance,
those who are 'oppressed', being affected by external occult
forces pressing in on them. There are also the 'obsessed', the
fascinated who stand at the doorway to the occult and are
addicted to some 'soft' form of it.

Bearing all this in mind, what then does it mean to be
possessed? Many witches or magicians will vigorously deny
that they are taken over by evil spirits. On occasions, even
Christians will find it difficult to see how they are indwelt by
the Holy Spirit and every minister has come across the new
Christian who simply cannot understand what has happened
to him. The apostle Paul had the same problem and had to
wait three days before one of God's ministers came along
with an explanation (Acts 9). We need to remind ourselves
of our own make-up before we can reach an adequate
explanation.

The make-up of Man

Man is one, and yet made up of three ingredients – body,
mind and spirit. The ingredients are thoroughly bound
together into one consistency, as thoroughly as a cake mix.
But unlike a static, inactive 'dollop', the body, mind and
spirit dynamically react and counter-react with each other.
They are more like an 'oscillation' of three strands, always
mingling with, and affecting, each other. Thus we can
understand how psychosomatic illnesses can be caused. A
wounded mind or spirit may break out in a body rash,
or cause impotency or even manifest itself in temporary
paralysis. The good doctor will always be listening to his
patient while examining the physical problem.

Materialists maintain that man is merely a body; a

mechanism similar to the computerised word processor I am now using to type these words. If anything goes wrong, you press the right buttons, feed in the corrections through drugs or surgery and, hey presto, all should be well. There are not, however, too many pure materialists left these days. Most acknowledge that man must at least have a mind, otherwise there is no sensible explanation for the many times when the body does not respond to mechanical treatment. Man is not just a mechanical 'animal–body' guided by built–in instincts and programmed along set lines of behaviour, like the birds and the bees. He has that something extra; that capacity to control his instincts, to order things into a whole, and to allow new facts to be integrated into past experiences. He can think in time, space, quality and quantity and, most important of all, he is self-aware. Man knows that he is a man, whereas the birds and the bees merely exist and do the job for which they were programmed.

Christians, among others, take one more excursion in our tour of man's make-up. They identify the psyche or the deep 'I'. It is the realm investigated by Freud, who probed it for guilt repressions. Jung, more positively, looked in the subconscious for wholesomeness and health. The conscious mind of man, he declared, was but the tip of an iceberg, and the great part of the self was submerged. We have, for instance, the capacity to store information and some of this can be recalled at will. However, man finds it impossible to retrieve facts stored in the deeper vaults of his subconscious. We know that there is information there because something must exert influences on those behaviours we sometimes cannot explain. Here in the subconscious are the hidden forces which propel and retard us; producing repressions, dreams, inspirations, and those touches of occasional genius.

J Stafford Wright wrote, 'We are asserting that the contents (of the Unconscious) are not normally accessible to our consciousness. If we again speak in personal terms we may say that *I am* at an unconscious level, as well as *I am* body and conscious mind. . . .[7]

Man, therefore, is an 'I' not only on the conscious level but also in the deep subconscious, and it is at this second level that the Holy Spirit comes to dwell when we are given a 'new' spirit (John 3:6; 2 Corinthians 5:17). But Christians at first must accept the presence of the Holy Spirit by faith. The new Christian is not directly aware of his presence. The Spirit is perceived gradually by his effect on the Christian, by changes in behaviour, attitudes and values. The new spirit given to us by the Holy Spirit is not a complete change of being, for we know that we are still, in many respects, the same as we were in our pre-conversion days. The Holy Spirit rather renews the deep 'I' so that the behaviour patterns emanating from it change. The new Christian needs to seriously question his conversion if, over a period of time, he does not find his values and perspectives changing.

To receive the Holy Spirit, we must lower our independent defences and welcome him in. Each human being is his own defended castle, protected by the 'drawbridge' of self-preservation and the 'moat' of common-sense. We can, however, lower this 'drawbridge' in times of great need or boredom, or through plain curiosity. If by doing this we can invite the source of good into the depths of our beings, we can most certainly open ourselves up to a source of evil.

In short, the witch, chaos magician, modern-day sorcerer, medium, fortune-teller, astrologer, and all other practitioners of the occult, can become 'possessed' by demons and still be able to laugh at the idea, or dismiss it as Christian 'anti-propaganda'. The devil is not likely to announce the presence of one of his agents with a fanfare. But he will make himself known by his evil influence over a period of time. And this is usually when the Christian minister is called in to deal with the suicidally depressed, the confused and the possessed.

There are, of course, a number within the occult —
especially in satanism and witchcraft — who believe whole-
heartedly that they can be indwelt by unholy spirits. They
have, after all, issued a specific invitation to the devil and put
their souls up for sale.

4

The Path to Magic

A pagan corpse called Pete helps us to progress to the next stage of our journey through this underworld of mystery, magic and sad deception. We have seen that man yearns to be the god of his own destiny. Yet in many spheres of his environment – his own life, philosophy, world affairs, religion and family – he is out of control, manipulated by a force which he chooses to treat as a joke, or dismiss as an artificial creation. We have acknowledged the far-from funny reality behind the music-hall caricature of the devil. We have looked at his long-term strategy, at the existence of his army of agents, and we have analysed the reasons for the rise in neo-paganism and the occult. We will shortly investigate the individual expressions of modern paganism, but first we need to delve into the mists shrouding its origins.

We start with Pete, a helpful 'guide' to the past. It was August 1st, 1984. Peat-bog worker Andy Mould picked a lump of matter from the elevator belt of the peat-shredding machine and threw it across to a workmate. As it hit the ground, the loose peat crumbled away to reveal a human foot.

Further investigation by police, forensic experts and archaeologists unearthed valuable clues which help us to peer through the mists of pagan and magical antiquity. The foot belonged to the remarkably well-preserved corpse of a man who had been murdered on what we know today as Lindow Moss, near Wilmslow in Cheshire. Lindow Man – Pete Marsh as the press promptly christened him – was one of the most complex examples of 'over-kill' that archaeologists had ever met. Don Brothwell, the biological adviser on the Lindow investigation, wrote, 'It is as if almost all the methods of killing someone had been encapsulated in this one individual.'[1]

Pete Marsh had a fractured skull, his throat had been cut, there was evidence of possible stab wounds in the chest, his neck was broken in two places and he had also been garrotted. Brothwell suggested it was 'the sort of violence which perhaps made sense as part of a complex ritual. . . .'[2]

It is feasible that this 300B.C. Lindow man – in his late twenties and possibly a well-manicured aristocrat fallen on hard times – was sacrificed to the gods of the day. First-century Roman historian Tacitus reported that certain northern tribes, who worshipped Mother Earth, were in the habit of dispensing with undesirables by pressing them down under a wicker hurdle into the slimy mud of a bog. Human sacrifices, even as late as Tacitus' day, were still part of the pagan lifestyle.

Pete Marsh was a product of a long reign of pagan gods, witchcraft and magic. His ancestors were often awe-struck as tremors gorged and then uplifted the earth beneath their feet. There were dangers in the vast forests which once covered our islands, and it was safer to live high on the heaths and moors, or in natural clearings by the rivers. But even there, gales and lightning and the incredible power of floodwaters could strike with fearful suddenness. It was these experiences which began to put the fear of gods into their primitive hearts.

Within prehistoric men was an innate urge to worship. In their own intelligence and in their striving for security and purpose, they must have suspected a super-intelligence, an all–powerful cause. The fact of their existence and the often-terrifying world around them was itself a natural revelation of something, or somebody, greater. But rather like our modern scientists, they were more interested in explaining what caused the immediate natural phenomena rather than in who created nature itself. Survival was the immediate essential, and so they had to find some way in which nature could be controlled . . . or even appeased. There developed a reverence for the wind, the towering trees, and the hills and mountains which dwarfed them. Gradually, to each element, plant, rock and stream a power was attributed. To the power was added personality as man fashioned gods out of his fear. The power-personalities were deified, and man began to worship the 'created rather than the Creator' (Romans 1:25). Animism or paganism was born, and man imprisoned himself in the fear of spirits. Some were good, many bad, but all demanded servitude and sacrifices.

Living on their wits and courage, men, women and children struggled to exist alongside and under nature; living so closely to it that they felt almost one with it. They would have had a highly-developed awareness . . . an animal sense to foresee danger beyond hearing and eyesight; a sense to determine friend or foe, and to discern the life-sustaining herbal gifts of nature as well as its poisonous curses. As pre-historic man began to cope more and more with his environment, his wisdom began to be collected and stored by the wise ones, later to become known as the wicca people.[3] Worship of nature became a manipulation of its forces through rituals, sacrifices, chants and hymns to the spirits. This religion gained sophistication in later centuries when farming people began to arrive from across the channel, bringing with them livestock, seed corn and an even richer understanding of the hidden ways and worship of nature. Soon strong, warlike races began to invade; warriors of bronze who easily subdued the flint-age Britons. Then came the men of iron, the Celts, with their ploughs and oxen, sickles and scythes opening up and cultivating the vast woodland areas. They too brought with them a more expansive world view of the magical ways used to direct the environment and influence friend or foe.

Our Lindow man was born into a community which had learned that the natural world could be partially subdued, levered and directed by the forces of divination and magic. He would have had a healthy respect for the magicians and sorcerers, the witchdoctors of paganism, who used their occult knowledge to compel or persuade gods, demons and spirits to do their will.

Bewitched by Baal

Here begins a bewitching tale; a love story which came to grief because of a bride drawn away by the false magnetism of paganism. It is a short story of the times we have dealt with, but is becoming increasing relevant to today's pagan scene.

The romance blossomed in the desert and the bride found herself walking down a well-prepared, and often miraculous 'aisle'. It came to an end in the foothills which snuggled in the shadow of a towering Mount Sinai, and it was here that God exchanged vows with his chosen partner. He had just saved her from the clutches of the Egyptians and a fate worse than death, and had promised to love, comfort, honour and keep her. In return, the bride had vowed to love, cherish and to obey, and there was not even a mention of 'till death do us part'. This was to be for ever!

They spent their honeymoon touring in the wilderness. Later, God carried his bride across the threshold of the River Jordan and into Canaan. This was to be her home, for he had long promised that she would live in a land overflowing with milk and honey.

The bride had hardly settled in before she began flirting with the local playboy called Baal. She saw him as the big-spender type, for he looked as though he had provided all that his Canaanite worshippers needed.

Baal came along at just the right time for God's none-too-faithful bride. Israel was beginning to have second thoughts about her husband. Oh, he might have worked wonders during the desert honeymoon. The daily delivery of manna had proved him to be a good breadwinner. But how would he measure up to the new situation in Canaan? It was a whole new lifestyle. Previously, wandering Israel had thought the ground was made for walking on. Now she had to dig it – or die! She was as much at home down on the farm as a burly Liverpool docker picking daisies.

Israel's husband might be able to provide bread, but could he be trusted to produce a thousand fields of corn? And what about the hundreds of vegetable patches, not to mention the many vineyards that would be needed to keep hunger and thirst at bay? Her very life was at stake! Could her husband be trusted to provide for her?

Baal, on the other hand, seemed quite the bright boy for the new situation. The conquered Canaanites seemed to be on a winner with him. Their kitchen pantries were over-flowing with good food, and there was plenty for everyone. Israel was tempted to walk out on her husband there and then, and throw in her lot with Baal. However, she decided to play it smart. She kept God as her husband and made Baal her lover.

Three thousand years later, we can still identify this twist in the eternal triangle. Today, we call it the Religious Insurance Game, and the modern version goes something like this: you put your money on God for Sundays, weddings and funerals. After all, they are his speciality. But when it comes to the video and a new car for the wife, you bank on the god of materialism.

Israel's version concerned more basic things. She kept her husband safely in the background and tried to keep him happy with a few prayers and sacrifices. But when it came to the bread-and-butter issues of daily living, she ran to her lover, Baal. For example, take the problem of rain – Israel's most vital need. In her new sun-blistered homeland, a long hot summer could last for years. If anyone could promise rain, he was at once a favourite. Baal claimed to do just that, and Israel fell for it. It was as tempting as a crate of Pepsi in the middle of the Sahara Desert!

The Canaanites used powers of suggestion to encourage Baal. Voodoo witchdoctors still practise similar occult arts by jabbing pins into effigies of their enemies. The Canaanites, however, were more interested in preserving life, and they had a much more enjoyable method of securing that end. Their aim was to encourage new life in Mother Earth. If they produced new life in the wombs of the sacred prostitutes in the local temples, surely Baal would get the message. A prostitute a day would keep the drought at bay.

This may have been just a great excuse for sex on demand for some nominal Baal worshippers.[4] Yet, whatever their motives, the majority were happily hooked on this pagan superstition. It was so potent that Israel soon became addicted.

Unfortunately, our story does not have a happy ending. At least, not an immediate one. Divorce and exile from the promised homeland were inevitable when God's love showed its tough side. The whole sad tale is told in the story of Hosea and his handling of Gomer, his wayward bride. The prophet told Israel that God would pour out his 'wrath on them like a flood of water' and that they would be 'trampled in judgment' because they were 'intent on pursuing idols'. Hosea called on them to repent, and then God would 'heal their waywardness and love them freely'. His anger would be turned away (Hosea 5:11–12; 14:4).

God's heart may be hard on the outside but it has a soft centre. God in his love also promised that Israel and he would be reunited eventually. It was the same almighty love that was later prepared to take human form in Jesus Christ to be a sacrifice for our sins (John 3:16).

5

Magical Thought

A Christian converted from satanism spoke to me of a London occult group whose members are made up of high-ranking civil servants, top industrialists and prominent city figures. He himself had been involved in an elite Home Counties group. Others in the occult assure me that each city and major town has its own small exclusive coven made up mostly of people in the professions. I asked one leading magician how many occultists there were in his home town of Blackpool.

'Between two and three hundred,' he shrugged. After a moment's thought he added, 'Those are the really committed ones.'

A Swiss baron, one of the world's richest men, puts his financial wizardry down to magic and witchcraft. 'The tarot cards,' he said, 'tell me whether I should fly on certain planes, or whether a party will be boring.' His magical intuition also tells him 'the right time to buy and sell'. An up-market group of occult magicians formed a consortium to play the stock-market using various methods of divination. They had no worries about their excellent progress until they decided to convert all their stocks into gold on 14th October, 1987. They divined that a massive slump was on the cards. Four days later, the greatest-ever stock-market collapse wiped billions off share prices.

I used to be amazed at the involvement of so many leading citizens in a field which popular opinion has traditionally reserved for eccentrics, freaks and 'old women' of both sexes. How was it possible, I used to wonder, for the city gent to swop his day-time brolly for a nocturnal Solomonic wand, stained with dragon's blood?[1] How could a close associate of mine programme a multi-national computer one minute, and the next be calculating the correct correlation of ritual paraphernalia, incenses, aromatic oils, and talismans? Is it possible to lead such a double life?

The simple answer is: no!

That's life!

The first principle of the occult is that it is a 24-hour-a-day occupation. These pillars of society are magicians, witches and satanists who just happen to be stockbrokers, teachers or computer geniuses. They live magic – think, breathe and eat it. From initiation onwards, it affects their whole lifestyle.

How can professional people commit what looks to us like intellectual suicide by being involved in such a bizarre capriciousness?

I suppose I could simply state that the devil is a pastmaster at blinding and misleading even the brightest brains. I could go on to explain that magic is no area for fools, and that the devil has provided a system which will satisfy all levels of thought. Both these statements would be true, but they would not do justice to the occultist's mind nor our understanding of it. If we are to approach them with love, we need an understanding of what makes them tick.

There can be no appreciation of paganism and the various paths of magic until we have tackled the thoughts which have landscaped them. It will be impossible to discern between what is popularly known as white magic (*theurgy*) and black magic (*goety*). There can be no comprehension of the combination of the two, goetic theurgy, one of the main paths of traditional magic.[2] We shall be lost in attempting to evaluate the other three main paths: witchcraft (paganism), yoga/meditation, and satanism/devil-worship. The latest and most influential trend, chaos magic – a liberal cannibalising of all paths – will be just a mesmerism of mumbo-jumbo to those not grounded in the source of all magic. So too will be the paranormal, New Age thinking, astrology, horoscopes and all that is to follow. We need to look at the underlying theories and try to understand.

At the heart of the occult are two issues: the location of reality, and the identity of the force which powers it.

A question of reality

Some years ago I used to play a game with my children which we called 'Upside-down land'.[3] It went something like this.

'In Upside-down Land, Rolls-Royces cost a penny, drunken elephants see pink men, and flies walk!' The next to go would try to be even more ridiculous.

However, though the game was unrealistic, it was totally logical – once we had accepted the first principle that everything was the reverse of reality.

The magician has a similar game. He does not play it. He lives it. It is deadly serious. As with the children's game, it does entail making one basic assumption: what we see, hear, taste, touch and smell is an illusion. Within us is reality.

'Occult science is the basic knowledge of the true man,' writes R G Torrens. 'Our working life is illusion; our inner life is truth. To those familiar only with external conscious impressions this may seem fantastic. . . .'[4]

The occultist turns his world inside-out. He maintains that what we see as reality is merely 'an illusion created by the impact of light vibrations on our senses and the interpretation of our senses'.[5]

To be fair, this idea is not without an argument. Atomic science and the more-recent quantum physics have shown us that objects which we once thought to be solid are, in fact, full of space. For instance, each of the billions of tiny atoms which make up this page you are now reading is, on one level, as spacious as our galaxy with its 'stars and planets' made up of protons, electrons, neutrons, and even things called quarks. The book as a whole makes up a vast universe. We are told that what we see is just a mass of energy and vibrations. Consequently, it is not real.[6] Reality is only within us, in the centre of our beings. The occult is therefore the 'science' of understanding reality as found in the inner man.

We could spend time analysing this quaint philosophy of reality, but we have space only to point out the inconsistency of the occultist's assumption. It can be stated simply.

The occultist makes a statement of faith when he turns his world inside-out. He has no firm evidence to prove that what he calls reality is indeed reality. He has no authority to make his judgment. It may sound like a brilliant philosophical and intellectual hypothesis. But at the end of the argument he is simply guessing. It is a statement of faith. He has no more chance of proving it than I have of disproving it.

At the heart of the occult is a guessing game!

We also need to say that a solid is no less a reality simply because modern man finds it to be full of holes. This merely adds to our understanding of what 'solid' is. Its structure and space actually add facts to its reality.

So why do highly intellectual people play their guessing game?

It works!

The Swiss baron knows it. His billions are sufficient proof for him. The hard-headed intellectual magicians I have met are equally convinced. An ex-satanist-turned Christian gave several instances of what his considerable powers had achieved.

The question which remains to be answered is: Why?

The identity of the force

The occultist, again through faith and guesswork, maintains that he is manipulating a natural energy within himself and the universe. This energy goes under many names, depending on which branch of the occult is involved. They include *life-force, life-essence, prana* (breath of life or life-principle), *etheric* (the force that lends substance to life), *kundalini* (spiritual energy, said to be a serpent of fire curled around the base of the spine), *ley lines* (so-called invisible currents of force coursing through our planet), *Brahma* (the energy-consciousness of our solar system), *od* (the magnetic force), *celestial hierarchies* (a chain of spiritual beings), *sakti* (energy of the gods), *silent watchers* (masters of outer space who allegedly help man's evolution), *elemental essence* (a formless essence reflecting the sum of all human thought), and *yin* and *yang*, forces which are said to form the basis of world order. Yin is feminine and mother of earth, and yang is masculine, a father force linked with the cosmic forces.[7]

The confusing variety of names is the occultist's major problem: he does not know what he is actually dealing with. He cannot even decide on its proper name or characteristics. Again, we are into guesswork.

The occultists might be confused as to the identity of what they are dealing with, but they can agree on one thing: the force, by whatever name, is generally neutral. It is neither good nor bad; neither black nor white. Many, especially in occult advertising, still employ terms like black and white magic, but the purist magician disapproves. He prefers to think of magic as a neutral force which can be put to good or bad use, rather as electricity can either warm or electrocute.

A black or white use of the force is determined only by the motives of the operator.

It also needs to be understood that though the occultist regularly refers to spirits, demons, devils and gods, these are meant only as personifications of the force, or the force within his own subconscious.

Not all in the occult are convinced that the powers are neutral. Several to whom I have spoken confessed, when pressed on the matter, that they are not sure.

'I would have said to you before that there was one energy,' said a Manchester high priestess. 'But, having thought that, there are overriding destructive elements . . . and they *are* overriding! I don't think they come from the same source. So, in that context, I do accept that there is a dual principle somewhere.'

Is there really a neutral force within us and throughout the universe, as modern occultists insist? May the force really be with us, as the *Star Wars* film assured millions in glorious techicolor? Is it a question of letting ourselves go so that this force can control us and our environment? The Christian needs answers when he approaches the occultists with love.

1. *Power needs a personal source:* there can be no power without personality.

'There are plenty of manifestations of power in society without personalities being at all obvious,' writes Michael Green, 'but they are there all the same. There cannot be power apart from an originating intelligence, planning it, calling it into being, using it.'[8]

The occultists may counter by reminding us of neutral forces such as electricity, magnetism and gravity. But my reason insists that there must be a personality behind even these forces. To believe that these are accidents is to say that there is no reason or design behind our world. And yet the world is full of reason and design. It is unreasonable to insist that the world's reason comes from non-reason. In a world in which every effect has a cause, it is reasonable to accept that the effect of the world has an intelligent cause. Our world demands a designer for it is so obviously designed. It also requires a 'prime mover' who has created and maintains movement, and consequently force.

2. *The unknown god of the occult:* The occultists do not know the identity of the power they manipulate. This is obvious from their total inability to agree on its name and characteristics. The Christian is therefore in a similar position to Paul when he met the men of Athens at the Areopagus (Acts 17:22f.). The apostle proclaims to them the identity of their unknown god as 'the God who made the world and everything in it ... the Lord of heaven and earth ... he himself gives all men life and breath and everything else'. Paul goes on to say that God 'has given proof of this to all men by raising him (Jesus) from the dead'.

The Christian likewise needs to introduce the occultist to Jesus, crucified and risen. Some will sneer, as Paul discovered. But others will say, 'We want to hear you again on this subject' (Acts 17:32).

3. *Only one power:* God's word knows of only one supreme source of power, and that is God himself (Genesis 1; Psalm 148:5). To give consideration to any other power is to worship that which has been created (Romans 1:25). There is, therefore, no other independent, neutral power. Nature itself is under God's control (Job 38:4f). All power and creation had to come through Jesus (Colossians 1:16). Even Jesus acknowledged that he had no power within himself apart from the Father (John 5:19).

As for Satan, the Bible allows him a lesser and limited power (Job 1:12; Luke 10:17,18; John 12:31,32; Ephesians 1:21). By definition, the devil, a created being, cannot be more powerful than the One who created him.

The reality of our world then is of one almighty and supreme power – God. He is the power-house of all good. He cannot mislead his creation to worship another part of creation, such as nature. He cannot possibly entice mankind to worship make-believe gods or unknown forces, for that would be against his will (Exodus 20:1–6). Satan, however, loves to abuse his permitted power and is ever willing to lead men and women in the wrong direction. He does this partly through the occult and paganism.

4. *Misuse of power condemned:* the manipulation of power through magic, sorcery and other forms of the occult is always condemned.

'Magic is a rival to true religion', states J Stafford Wright. 'True religion centres on the personal experience of the one true God, with an attempt to live a life that is conformable to His will. The believer walks humbly with God, prays to Him, and is prepared to accept the circumstances of life as the sphere in which to glorify Him. Magic, on the other hand, deals with lower supernatural beings, or attempts to force issues by using psychic forces, irrespective of whether the issues are for the glory of God.'[9]

God, through his servants, continually condemned the magicians of Egypt, who imitated the wonders which Moses performed (Exodus 7: 11; 2 Timothy 3:8).[10] He hated witchcraft and the illusions of Jezebel and Manasseh (2 Kings 9:22: 21:6: Micah 5:12). The Lord abhorred mediums and those who contacted the dead, as outlined in the 'witch of Endor' story (1 Samuel 28. This is not the description of what we now call a witch, but rather a spiritist medium).

5. *A question of authority:* at the heart of the occult is a distaste for any authority.

'Be yourself!' one witch screamed at me as we talked. 'I feel like I'm talking to a book!' She wanted me to 'let myself go and forget the Bible'. Nor was she too happy about my 'obsession' with Jesus as the living Word of God. Her authority was herself, her feelings and emotions. For all practical purposes, she was her own god.

When ministering to those in the occult, it is vital to be sure of the foundations for your authority. It is often the first line of attack, and this is the main reason why a later chapter is devoted to a defence of Scripture.

6. *The thinking rebel:* 'Thinking,' as some wag once said, 'makes my brain hurt!' In today's 'instant coffee' society, western man dislikes the hard grind of thinking, and is often too impatient to wait for the process of percolation to yield a digestible idea. Modern life goes too fast to stop and think, and so we adopt the mass–manufactured thoughts from the 'telly' or make do with our own first-hand prejudices.

The occultist, including the majority of pagans, are rebels. They detest the prepacked convenience of our mad, mad world, and yearn to flip it into reverse and return to the old ways. They do this by applying the brakes of yoga, meditation, ritual magic, astrology and so on. Silvanus, a northern witch, put it this way:

> As plastic civilization encroaches, and more and more man–made scabs cover the earth, people are beginning to realise that they are not plastic people ... but flesh and blood people. Whereas before, they may have taken their earth for granted, now, because it is disappearing, they are feeling lost ... the whole artificial thing has given rise to a backlash, a return to paganism ... You are getting all sorts of experimental groups coming up trying to revive the spirit of paganism.[11]

A chaos magician, gathered with others around a bonfire on a derelict site, had no choice as to whether or not his world was slowed down. He was unemployed ...

'The devil finds work for idle hands to do,' he said, 'but whose fault is it that we're sat here twiddling our thumbs? We didn't ask for this situation. ... Sitting on your backside with nothing to do, you start using your mind – and why not?'[12]

Here, at last, the Christian, the occultist and the pagan find common ground. We are each of us in a battle against the twentieth century gods of materialism and humanism. Unfortunately, the pagan retreats backwards only as far as nature, and the occultist to the spirits behind nature (whether he deems them real or imaginary). The Christian goes further, to the One who created nature.

6

Chaos!

Chaos magic is the latest occult trend, and is about as dangerous as Russian roulette. In this magic of the eighties there are few safeguards, little control and total freedom to expand your consciousness, or blow it to kingdom come. This is the path of the 'spiritual warrior', the one who is prepared to risk everything for the sake of the prize. Greek mythology had its Argonauts gambling their lives to reach the Golden Fleece. Chaos magic has its 'psychonauts' willing to chance their sanity as they fling themselves into what they call 'the void'.

In case you feel this description is a little over the top, read what the chaoist himself has to say.

'Chaos magic is dangerous, awesome, full of potential and therefore mysterious . . . it has an ultra–sinister aspect to it . . . anyone can jump into the cauldron of chaos and discover powerful magic, and the only rules are those imposed upon oneself by one's own courage. . . . We specify our desire, open up our subjective will to render our reality malleable, and then throw ourselves on the mercy of the gods. This then is the danger of chaos magic. We prepare to sacrifice our identity and intellect in order to interface with the void. We give ourselves up to death.'[1]

Chaos magic is 'punk' magic. It is angry magic. It is a

reaction against all authority, tradition and leadership and is not bound by any moral or ethical standards. Its only law is: 'Do whatever you like; all things are permissible.' In some ways it is the occult outworking of the permissive society, with no holds barred.

The traditional forms of the occult, like witchcraft, and even satanism, have two features which give a slight measure of control and protection – morals and ritual. Some of the old occultic arts have a highly-developed ethic which could be summed up as 'Do unto others as you would have them do unto you.'[3] This dissuades the traditionalist magician from total anarchy. Rituals are designed to ensure that all things are done with order, and they act as a brake to protect the participants from chaos. But the new chaos magician throws everything, even himself, to the wind – or, more appropriately, into an uncontrollable vortex.

This is the frightening path of magic along which many are being led. It is the fastest-growing group in occult circles and is rapidly overhauling the traditional ways.

'In the early days when people entered the occult, 50% went into witchcraft,' explained a chaoist who makes occult paraphernalia for colleagues in Europe and the States. 'By the seventies, this figure had reduced substantially, and today only about 20% bother with wicca.'

The birth of chaos magic

The magicians have their own explanation of the origins of chaos, but first let me suggest a Christian perspective.

In every religious revival on record, it seems as though the Holy Spirit has created, or used, a special social environment to bring people back to God. Analyse the modern upsurge of Christianity in Korea, Indonesia, South America and the past renewals in our own isles, and there is always a special social 'sparking-point' for revival. Christian history lecturer Alan Gilbert pinpoints, for example, two contributory factors in the revivals of England and Wales in 1904–5: The political and sociological tension between church and chapel, and also the religious rebellion against the Tory Education Act of 1902.[4]

This may all seem a long way from today's 'occult revival', but there is a link. The social upheaval which began during the last war and continued afterwards, began to prise people loose from the traditions of the past. The political, theological and sociological rituals and authorities lost their power to hold and guide the masses. Disenchantment with a war-torn, bloody past flooded into the up-and-coming generation and exploded in college-campus riots, and inspired the rebellion of rock, long hair and flower-power.

'Give love a chance,' was the cry, and the type of love of which they sang encouraged an era of liberty and permissiveness. The church, always late to catch up with modern trends, was hit in the sixties with a mini-revival based on the mood of the era.

The charismatic movement was born. At this point, please do not misunderstand. I believe that the charismatics, in their new-found liberty, have often produced the true fruit of the Holy Spirit. Some may have caused schisms and upheavals, but they have been responsible for a new freedom from the crushing traditions of the past, and liberated many churches from deadening, Spirit-sapping rituals. The charismatics excel in experiencing the dynamic power of the Holy Spirit as he blows in many and varied ways. They focus on the use of Spirit-gifted people in their fellowship and have a healthy view of the body of Christ.

They do have their weaknesses though. There is a general discomfort with dogma, and a tendency to be led, not so much by Scripture, but by their own subjective feelings based on what they believe to be the Spirit's inner guiding. Some can also find themselves too busy with arm-raising exercises to lift a hand in Christian service. I stress that this is a generalisation, and in recent years they have improved the balance between personal experience, feelings and the authority of Scripture.

It has been well-said that the devil is 'the ape of God'. Whatever the Holy Spirit produces,' Satan will endeavour to reproduce. I have come to believe that chaos magic is his inferior copy-cat of the charismatic movement. The very essence of chaos magic is a strong dislike of the doctrines and dogmas of the past, a freedom from any restraints, and a magic securely grounded on 'what feels right'.

The Christian charismatics know that they are involved in an often alarming and sometimes precarious, but always exciting, adventure with God. They also have faith in a loving God whose everlasting arms will catch them should they fall. They walk the high-wire with a safety net. The 'chaos charismatics' likewise live dangerously but without the protection that the Christian enjoys. The chaoists fly into their 'void' on a trapeze of cotton strings knowing that if the weight is too much, they may never come back! Note what they themselves say about reaching into the 'void' to satisfy their desires.

> If we are wise, then the changes we desire in our reality are small ones, and the requirement puts a small strain on the universe. We return to this dimension with our consciousness changed in important areas. We are expanded, yet still identifiable as the person before. There is a point of no return, however. If the point of no-return is reached, our plasma-will is simply absorbed by the greater whole, and we cease to exist. We revert to god. Those who demand too much in their magic can return a lunatic, or may end up being absorbed by it altogether. The spiritual warrior has the courage to take this path, for psychonauts find the prize worth the risk.[5]

Chaos magic can be traced back to the first half of our century, and the experiments and explorations of Aleister Crowley. He adopted ancient eastern magic and extracted and refined it to provide a structure of techniques which would be understandable to the modern western mind. At the same time Austin Spare was making intellectual sense out of eastern Shamanism,[6] and introducing magicians to the concept of 'a void'. More modern magicians began to experiment with these newer ideas, some trying them out in drug-induced states. Others introduced fresh ideas loosely based on the quantum theory, neurosurgery and nuclear physics. An 'anything goes' mentality was simultaneously being developed, and one of the facets to go was secrecy. Magic was rescued from the idle weathy and the eccentric academics and bestowed on the modern society of leisure by publishers ever-watchful for a new market. Commerce introduced the occult to those with time on their hands, and the new initiates extended the experimentation process to introduce an 'anarchy' more in keeping with the world around them. They were prepared to take only what they considered to be the cream of old magic and refused any suggestions of order and philosophy. It developed into chaos with everybody doing what they wanted, and chaos magic became its name by popular usage.

We don't need evangelists!

A chaos magician scoffed at Christian claims that he was leading youngsters and immature adults astray. First, he did not consider it was wrong to introduce people to his field, and secondly, he added, 'The occult has never needed evangelists. There are always more people trying to get in than there are places.'

His comments, and those of others, concerning recruitment and membership are revealing.

We are not interested in taking in people unless they have some gift or potential . . . they must be able to contribute to the power of the group. Chaos magic is not a charity. If we are going to invest time in training newcomers, we want a dividend at the end.'

This came from the chaoist who made the occult paraphernalia.[7]

All the following techniques can be dangerous to those who are nervously inclined or who are chronically ill or those with high-blood pressure or heart trouble. People who use heart-pacemakers and pregnant women should under no circumstances follow any of the training schedules given on this tape ... all experiments are undertaken at your own risk ... [8]

The spiritually-inclined people generally end up in wicca, and the more sceptical come to us (chaos magic) ... the academic sorts are told to go into sociology and leave us alone. The power-mad, the mentally ill and those who are generally unstable, we send to the Pentecostals. They accept them because nobody else will .... – A chaos magician.

More and more people are feeling alienated from a civilisation that has lost its mystery and meaning, and seems to be bent on an ecological or nuclear disaster course. ... Christianity seems to be able to offer no better an option than sitting back quietly and accepting it ... and waiting for something better to happen hereafter. It seems a little more positive to hope that you can plumb your own depths and find some meaning and fulfilment while you're actually here. And we like to think that we offer that ... [9]

After all, if you are a born-again Christian and you really do believe that come the nuclear holocaust you'll be swept up in the rapture to heaven, then you really won't be doing that much to stop it. In fact, you'll be rather looking forward to it. I think a more pagan or occult world view tends to be a life-supporting and life-enhancing world view, which is better than the predominantly death-orientated world view of the Christian .... [10]

There are several points we need to consider:
1. *Chaos magic is primarily a solo path:* it is personal, between the student magician and the 'void'. He is well on his way

before he attempts to join a group. He has either made it, or the 'void' has 'unmade' him.

2. *The selective magicians are not typical:* Chaos magic will and does take in all-comers. The 'choosy' magician quoted was in at the very birth of chaos magic. For him and his advanced colleagues to accept novices would be like me being selected to play for the European Ryder Cup golf team. I am, however, quite at home with other golfing 'rabbits'. The local chaoists will also find that the same is true for them. Incidentally, because chaos magicians deride any authority or leadership, the budding chaoist ends up with more chaos than he bargained for. He is left alone in a highly dangerous area, and is about as safe as a toddler riding his tricycle round Silverstone on Grand Prix day!

3. *Chaoism reflects modern self-centredness:* the chaoist claims that his way is life-supporting and life-enhancing. It is, however, only for himself that he claims it. He is not here to enhance the lives of others. After all, as they say, they are not a charity. The weak, the ungifted, the lunatics and the unstable are cast aside as unsuitable. Thank God for Christians who are prepared to take in all-comers, fit or failing.

4. *A criticism that hits home:* how would you answer the charge that Christians are just sitting back waiting for heaven, unconcerned as to whether or not they leave planet earth naturally or via a nuclear explosion?

I think some would have no alternative but to plead guilty! True, many of us pray for peace; many of our leaders are hard at work quietly working out that prayer in numerous ways. Many local churches do try to reach into their surrounding communities to enhance life for those in need. But are we really doing enough? One of Jesus' major commissions to his followers was to feed the hungry, visit the sick and look after those in prison. 'Whatever you do for these needy people, you do for me' (Matthew 25:31–46). Many Christians take that command seriously – but not all!

And it is a major part of the teachings of Christ. It is so important that it determines how we are classed – as sheep to follow our Father into heaven, or as goats who take the left-hand path.[11]

5. *A criticism way off target:* Christianity stands accused of being death-orientated; that it does not enhance or support life. I can only assume that the chaoists who make this charge have only experienced 'churchianity' rather than true Christianity. 'Churchianity' has corpse-like clergy whose white robes remind one of disenchanted chanters. Every service is as cheerful as a funeral, and the congregation only smile when their dreadful duty is done.

True Christianity has its serious side but also involves laughing with joy and holding hands with the Number One Person in the universe. It is being in love with Jesus who loved us so much that he gave his life and rose again to give a new way of living. Often a service can become a celebration; an adulation and a coronation as the King of kings is crowned yet again with the praise of his people.

True Christianity knows nothing of a 'void'. It knows only of a heart vaster than the universe; a love that wants to pump the richness of real and abundant life into those who crave purpose, peace and fulfilment. The true Christian is commanded to go out of his way to invite others to enter life in all its fullness (John 10:10).

6. *The sadness of chaos:* the chaoist's hope is to plumb the depths of his being to find some meaning and fulfilment while on earth. What a desperately sad statement in comparison to that which Christ offers. How tragic to have to be satisfied with a glorified navel-gazing exercise, or to fling yourself into an inner void for God-only-knows what to affect you. Nestling as we do in the life-enhancing arms of Christ, does it not make you want to reach out to those in chaos?

7. The higher practitioners of chaos magic may feel they have no need of evangelists, but this is certainly not true for other branches of paganism and the occult. I have met many witches and satanists who are only too happy to enlist the curious, the troubled, and also any who are genuinely seeking for truth and purpose in life. Judging from the high numbers of secondary-school children involved in magic, the occult and paganism in my own area, evangelism starts with the young.

7

Witchcraft

The traffic patrolman signalled for the speeding lady driver to pull over. The events which followed put the police force of a large northern town on full alert for a missing officer.

The police driver asked for her documents but the woman explained, with a pleasant smile that they were at her home nearby. She invited him to follow her, and the officer took the unusual course of agreeing.[1] After a short run, the lady driver turned down a narrow lane, and then into the driveway leading to a large ranch-type bungalow. As the police officer followed, he saw two notices declaring, 'No entry. Trespassers will be prosecuted'. Two things made him slow down as he came to the entrance. The first was the knowledge that the bungalow was situated in the town's radio 'black spot' and he had failed to report where he was going. The second was the sight of strange mythological beasts and demonic gargoyles which surrounded and surmounted the gateway. Drawing to a halt, he recollected an investigation which one of his colleagues had conducted some weeks before. It had been something to do with a young girl being held against her will on a secluded stud farm, and there had been a mention of witchcraft and drugs. This, he now recalled, was the same place. He had laughed when told about the 'devil group with lots of surplus young girls hanging around'. Now he was not too amused as he stepped from his car beneath a large CB aerial flying a strange black flag engraved with a gold five-pointed star (an occult symbol).[2]

By this time, the woman had left her car and the officer followed her into the house. He noticed a picture of a furry creature with a goat's head and cloven hooves as they entered the sitting room.

'That's a bit ghoulish,' he joked nervously. 'Is it the devil?' The woman's strange reaction completely unnerved him.

'Her eyes began to roll and then the pupils disappeared upward,' he later told his superiors. 'She began to make weird, inhuman sounds and went as stiff as a board. And then the picture itself seemed to come alive.'

The picture incident proved too much for the officer and he decided to retire. He did so quickly, but went into the wrong room which was full of 'weird things'.

'I lost my bottle completely and ran,' he explained later. It was two hours before he felt sufficiently recovered to stop at a phone box and report in.

A short while after the alert had been called off for the missing officer, a CID friend contacted me to see if I could help with their 'enquiries'. Apparently, the owners of the ranch bungalow were suspected of being involved in the exhumation of bodies at two local churches when skulls and other bones were removed, and also the disappearance of three goats on or about the thirteenth of each of the previous three months. As I write, the police enquiries are still in progress.

Some days later, a farmer phoned to discover whether I knew the meeting times and places of witches in his area. For several months he had been finding rings of stones, surrounding a large boulder which was often topped with melted wax. On one occasion he had found a sheep's head jammed between some of the stones. There were entrails of an animal to be found in other parts of the circle. It sounded more like a satanist ritual until he revealed that he had caught several people naked the previous evening. Only witches normally practise their rituals 'skyclad', though other groups have been known to skip round in their birthday suits. The farmer had fired a warning barrel, but his only reward was a pair of trousers. The owner had bolted along with his fellow worshippers.

In fairness to witches, these two events are probably not typical. Modern witchcraft has as many 'denominations' as does Christianity and, just as a respectable high Anglo-Catholic might shrivel with embarrassment at the gregarious worship of black Pentecostals, and vice versa, there are similar reactions between various branches of witchcraft.

The great witch trials

In days of old, people of a village would meet to celebrate pagan festivals. As the influence of Christianity spread, the new religion gradually embraced and took over the festivals, giving them new names and meanings. For centuries, the two religions co-existed uneasily though there were inter-mittent purges on witches and people who insisted on celebrating their pagan heritage.

Serious persecution began to arise in the days of King Henry VIII who, at first, was fascinated by sorcery and witchcraft. He consulted diviners when Anne Boleyn became pregnant, anxious to know whether he could expect a male heir. The fascination was, however, accompanied by fear, and there seemed to be an inner conflict between his Christian beliefs and the sorcery of witchcraft. His spiritual advisers were none too happy with his reliance on pagan practices, nor probably was his court favourite Buckingham. There is evidence that a seer had foretold that, should Henry die without an heir, the earl would assume the throne. Buckingham lost his head over the matter.

By 1542, Henry's fear had become the dominant emotion

and he ordered Parliament to legislate against those who used incantations and practices of sorcery aimed at killing or injuring people, or destroying their goods and chattels. Daughter Elizabeth later refined the laws and increased the penalties, partly because she and her advisers often suspected that there were occult plots against the throne. For three hundred years the persecution of witchcraft was to continue until the advent of our modern scientific world. Witchcraft itself never became illegal (as on the continent where the Inquisition held sway), only the alleged effects, such as damage to goods, or death and injury to people. The first trial under the Witchcraft Act of 1563 was held in Chelmsford in 1566, when Agnes Waterhouse was hanged largely on the evidence of a small child. This was often to be a disturbing element in many of the subsequent trials when children's uncorroborated evidence sent many to prison and to the gallows.[3] Hundreds of trials followed all over the land in the wake of Chelmsford. There were the witches of Windsor, Northamptonshire, Bideford, Newbury, Burton, St. Osyth, Bilson and Faversham, to name but a few.

The Lancashire witches of Pendle were typical. The sorry story began on 18th March 1612, when a teenage beggar girl, Alizon Device, flew into a rage when a pedlar refused to give her some pins. As she walked away from him he suffered a stroke, and Alizon was later arrested and tried on the charge that she 'practised, exercised and used her devilish and wicked arts' and that by these she 'had him lamed so that his body wasted and consumed away'. It seems amazing today, and more especially because there was no torture in Lancashire, that Alizon confessed.[4] She said that a black dog had asked her, 'What would you have me do to this man?' She answered, 'Lame him!'

Alizon went on to blame 'Old Demdike', her grand-mother, and also incriminated others. Later, the evidence of nine-year-old Jennet Demdike was used against other adults, and all were taken for trial at Lancaster Assizes. On

18th August, the trial of nineteen witches, not all from Pendle, began. Some pleaded guilty while others were incriminated by the children's evidence, and two days later a dozen were hanged before thousands on the hill overlooking Lancaster Castle.[5]

The ready acceptance of children's testimony was not the only disturbing fact surrounding the executions. Consider also the hysterical witch-hunt mentality of the moral and upright Protestants, later to be personified in the form of the seventeenth-century Witch-finder General, Matthew Hopkins. Any individual with a socially unacceptable appearance might be suspected of witchcraft. One description of the typical witch declares as highly suspect 'women which be commonly old, lame, blear-eied, pale, fowle and full of wrinkles; poore, sullen, superstitious, and papists; or such as knowe no religion: in whose drousie minds the divell doth goten a fine seat'.

Looking back on the scant evidence we have to assume that, along with the guilty, some innocent men and women went to their deaths, despite their confessions.

Underground witchcraft

It was not until the later trials that the courts began to hear about 'covens' of witches. What had apparently happened was that, faced with persecution, the committed witches had formed themselves into small clandestine groups and became separated from each other. The covens were restricted to thirteen, possibly because they considered it unlucky for the enemy Christian church due to the number at the Last Supper. More probably it was to do with each member representing one of the lunar months of the year. Only the coven leaders had contact with each other to prevent infiltration of spies and to reduce the risk of others being incriminated should one of their number be arrested and interrogated. This separation actually continued into this century, and was only totally eradicated with the upsurge in witchcraft in the late fifties and early sixties.

'Churchmanships' of witchcraft

There are, broadly speaking, three types of witches. One witch described them to me in newspaper terms.

There are the *News of the World* types who enjoy the sensational, the sex and the thrills. Members of these covens are usually 'nominal' witches who pay only lip-service to the dogmas and are interested in it only for the kicks it provides. This type of coven is usually on the borderline of satanism, and the 'sincere' members believe that the devil and his demons need them as agents to wreak havoc in the world. The agents make a pact with the devil either privately or accompanied by great ceremony during one of the main sabbats of the year.[6] Whichever way, the devil will seal the pact for the usual price of his new agent's soul. On occasions, the pact is accompanied by sexual encounters. This type of witch is the most likely to desecrate 'sacred' property such as graveyards and churches, and to celebrate the black mass, which pokes fun at high church religion.

An ex-witch revealed that initiation ceremonies include the sacrifice of animals and the drinking of a 'cocktail' of animal and human blood and urine. In some instances, a woman will be ordered to become pregnant and the resulting baby will then be sacrificed. Male children are sacrificed by females and vice versa. When adults break a coven's sexual rules, the punishment can be death. The offender is sacrificed, with the 'officiant' being the one who was sexually offended. The heart can be removed and offered to Satan, after which the body is removed to another location and burnt beyond recognition.

There is growing evidence that this type of witch-satanist is involved in child abuse on a growing scale. In the two months prior to writing this chapter, my counselling has involved one thirteen-year-old babysitter for a coven who was drugged and sexually abused for two years before eventually plucking up the courage to tell her parents. A mother asked for help in rescuing her fourteen-year-old daughter from a coven. Three children in the North-east were taken into care and their parents and other adults were charged and found guilty of using them sexually in their rituals. One associate reported dealing with a mother in the Hull area who had refused to surrender her seven-year-old son to her coven. She was placed in a safe house but later returned to the coven of her own free will. She still refused to give up her son and instead was punished. The mother, who herself had been initiated at the age of five, felt unable to break away from the group. Another mother, from Burnley, spoke to me of her six-year-old son who was 'tampered with' by a witch in the neighbourhood. She spoke of many teenagers being involved with this witch. I asked for names and addresses so that I might pass on details to the police. The mother refused.

It was this type of information which led to an adjournment debate on child abuse and the practices of witchcraft in the House of Commons on April 27, 1988. Mr Geoffrey Dickens, MP for Littleborough and Saddleworth, announced that he would be presenting a dossier of evidence to the Home Office in due course. Mr John Patten, a junior minister in the Home Office, assured the House that he would gladly amend the law if necessary, and added his own warning that schools and parents should continue to alert their children against the dangers and perversions of cults. As we go to press, this matter is still under discussion.

Justice demands that I stress one important point. This type of physical abuse is limited to the more extreme forms of witchcraft and satanism. Other forms of the occult, I believe, certainly mislead and abuse youngsters spiritually and mentally, but it is unjust to accuse them of physical abuse.

The second type of witchcraft is what might be termed the *Guardian* newspaper class. These witches are the 'middle class' of respectability, always concerned to distance themselves from the first group and ever keen to present the acceptable face of natural religion. This group is the first to rise up in indignation and shout 'witch-hunt' and 'persecution' whenever Christians condemn the occult. These are the people who insist that, because the word 'occult' means 'hidden' the church is, by definition, also part of the occult. Christians, they complain, should refrain from criticism, and instead join with them for the good of each other and mankind in general.

The first group of witches are never concerned to defend their reputation. They are content to maintain their secrecy and carry on businss as normal. No so with the 'middle-class' witch.

'Join forces with us,' invited one witch called Ian, 'and try to understand us . . . try to find out what we really believe in. Obviously Christians know very little about us.'[7]

These are the witches who are dominant in the north of England. The 'blood and gore' witches appear to be strong in the South of England, especially in and around London. Our 'second-level' witch is probably quite a respectable member of the community and may meet with fellow members of the coven in a house down your street or on your estate. He and his associates[8] will even dedicate one of their rituals to the cause of understanding and the suspension of hostilities between 'our brothers and sisters who follow other paths of religion'.[9]

In this age of tolerance, it seems churlish to ignore so charitable an offer. But let us first examine their beliefs.

This form of witchcraft is a religion of the earth. The worshippers prefer to be known as followers of wicca; the wise ones who revere the natural life-force. They reject the Christian God whom they describe as 'a Father God standing outside everything and everyone'.[10] They prefer to personify the life-force as male and female, known variously as the God and Goddess, Lord and Lady, the Horned God and the Silver Lady among others. The female is always dominant as a Mother Earth concept, making witchcraft *the* matriarchal religion. They still retain large elements of animism, a belief which assigns a divine spark or spirit to every material thing. This religion often proves a great attraction to the romantic who is tired of concrete and high-power technology, and yearns for a return to nature. The coven will also employ magic, but this is only secondary to its beliefs and worship. The magic will be used in organised or private rituals for healing, and divination for guidance when important decisions loom. The leader or high priest(ess) is chosen for the quality of psychic power exhibited, and how open he or she is to the life-force. All members are believed to have the life-force within them, and they insist that only within themselves will they find what Christians call God.

It is difficult to find much in common between Christianity and witchcraft. In fact, our 'middle-class' witches appear to be similar to the Canaanites (see p. 56), whom God roundly condemned. Both religions not only put other gods before the one true God, they even fail to acknowledge his existence. Wiccans therefore break the first commandment of a group with which they wish to work (Exodus 20:3).

Wicca followers, like the Canaanites, visualise their gods as images of animals or horned gods, thus breaking the second commandment of the group with whom they seek closer ties (Exodus 20:4).

The witches, as the followers of Baal, take the attributes and names of God and give them to other powers or to false gods. They also fail to set aside a holy day for God. In doing these two things, they tear up the third and fourth commandments of the Christian faith (Exodus 20:7,8). Finally, they would not be too keen on obeying the seventh commandment concerning adultery and abuse of sex

(Exodus 20:14). I explained this last point to one witch and he said that the same could be said for Christianity. It was the week that the Church of England's General Synod had agreed that homosexuality was a sin but had refused to discipline the sinner.[11]

However, before these 'middle class' witches invite Christians to work with them, it would seem that it is they who really need to 'try and understand us and get to know what we believe'. Christians would be forced to tear up half their commandments before unity could be achieved.

The third group of witches could be likened to the *Daily Telegraph* end of the spectrum. These are the isolated witches; the hermits or ascetics of the occult. They reject the first group for being too sensationalist, for being concerned only with 'blood, gore and thrills'. They insist that this group is 'nominal', rather like Christians who go to church for the comfortable feelings they get, but who never put their faith into practice. The 'middle-class' witches are dismissed by the ascetics as a 'weird bunch of ecology freaks'.

This third group of mystics are apparently disenchanted ex-coven members who have grown tired of the 'back-biting and bitchiness' in the occult. They also tend to practise paths of magic which require solitude. Some of the work of Gerald Gardner, and much of Aleister Crowley's magic, can only be satisfactorily practised in privacy and seclusion.

Satanism

A London Christian, who had spent fifteen years in many branches of the occult before his conversion at the Luis Palau mission at Queens Park Rangers soccer stadium in 1985, said: 'In my experience, there are not too many differences between the first group of witches and satanists. You might say they are two levels of the same thing, like the high and low churches of Christianity.'

There is, however, a distinctly religious form of satanism which states that Christianity has got the facts all wrong. Satan is really the true Son of God and Jesus is the usurper.

'The popular image of Satan is of this great evil force that can destroy anything,' explained a satanist adorned with the title of High Priest of the Northern Order of the Prince. 'We don't believe in evil and bad, contrary to what the popular media say. We have a special code of ethics that we have to follow. They are exacting and good, and they apply to everyday life. All our fans are happy. We teach people to look after themselves and how to heal . . . we've got to keep hidden because of the persecution we get through certain people who go on propagating this evil entity of Satan.'

It was interesting to talk with a family who belonged to this high priest's group and hear their side of the story. They had come to me for help in extricating themselves from satanism because the high priest had insisted on performing the 'Act of Unity' with their fourteen-year-old daughter. The mother had pointed out that her daughter was under the legal age for sexual intercourse, but the high priest had explained that the order had its own calendar. According to this, the daughter was now nineteen years old. The father of the family was not so much concerned about his daughter as about the 'Acts of Unity' he himself was ordered to perform on the temple's Altar of Initiation.

'It wasn't fair,' he complained. 'The high priest got all the young good-looking ones while I was left with the old fat ones.' The father's real purpose in allowing me to visit the family was not so much to get help, but to recoup the £40 he had spent on satanist scriptures, which he wanted to sell to me. When I refused to buy them, he lost interest. His daughter summed up the real emotions of herself and her mother.

'We were supposed to follow our scriptures,' she explained, 'but all he [the high priest] did was to change them or make extra things up to suit what he wanted to do.'

This group represents a small minority of satanists. They are dismissed by others in the occult, who claim that the group 'tell outsiders this tall story (of Satan being the Son of God) to make themselves look respectable'. These groups use either a re-written version of the Bible or ancient occult documents originating in Egypt, called the Raz Cathab Mishael (one of several spellings). Historically speaking, neither their bastardised bible nor their own scriptures have any authority whatsoever.

We now turn to one woman's battle with satanism – a mother's fight for her son who was offered to Satan only hours after his birth. The names and some of the details have had to be changed to protect those involved.

8

A Mother's Story

Real-life narratives never have beginnings. But it is at least necessary to start Mary's story on the morning of Tuesday, 12th January 1937, when she was fifteen years old. It was a moment of horror in a childhood lived on the edges of the occult east of London.

At that time, Mary's mother had a strange, possessive relationship with another woman; an affair which young Mary was only just beginning to understand. Both women arrived without warning one morning at the home of Mary's grandfather, which had been the girl's permanent home. Mary had been looked after by a nanny until the age of seven and had then stayed intermittently with elderly relatives. Her mother could not be bothered with her.

The two women had barely crossed the threshold before they were halted in their tracks.

'Get that woman out of my house,' grandfather shouted from his sick bed. 'I don't want her under my roof.' Both women immediately turned on their heels without a word and left. Mary wrote of the incident later,

'My grandfather had signed his own death warrant, though only my mother knew it at the time.' The local doctor had got into the habit of calling after his morning surgery, not that there was much need. Grandfather was only suffering from a nagging cough and mild flu but he was, after all, somewhat of a grandee in the town because of his wealth. On that Tuesday morning my mother came with the doctor and took him to a spare bedroom, leaving the door ajar. I was passing when I noticed a large roll of money in notes pass into the doctor's hand.

'"How long will it be?" I heard my mother ask.

'"About half an hour," the doctor replied.

'I went on down the corridor to see my grandfather, wondering what it was that would take half an hour. I noticed the clock on the mantlepiece and it was 10.15. The doctor followed me almost immediately and injected my grandfather in the back of his hand. He then went downstairs, and I heard my mother join him. I stood at the foot of the bed and watched my grandfather go to sleep. A little later, he took his last breath.

'It suddenly came to me what they had done. I looked at the clock and it was 10.40. Strangely, I had no sense of panic, only a feeling of guilt. I felt as though I should have done something.'

Mary was still standing by the bed when her mother came into the room and, without looking at the bed, walked over to where grandfather kept his emergency money, usually about £1,000. It had already dawned on the girl that, from this moment on, she was on her own, and that there was nobody to stand between her and whatever might be devised for her in the future. Her only chance of survival, she felt, was to keep a tight rein over her feelings and words.

Her mother announced that she was now going to her lady friend and put grandfather's money in her bag. 'Get in touch with the undertakers and make all the arrangements. Sampsons will do the cards. Let me know the time of the funeral.'

Mary was not in the least surprised. That had been the way of things for several years. Whenever a crisis loomed, her mother would often turn on her off-spring and demand to know what she was going to do about it. She was so disorganised and absent-minded that, while out visiting, she would often forget that she had a daughter, leaving her stranded for hours.

Following the funeral, Mary stayed on at her grand-father's home on her own, or occasionally with distant relatives. For several years, she had not been attending school regularly but had instead been sent on provincial theatre tours, first with a dancing troupe and later as a violinist or actress. Mother, in the meantime, had supplied the school inspector with countless sick notes, always pro-vided by her tame doctor. The otherwise lonely mid-teen years were made bearable with the presence of Terry, a third cousin whom she had known since she was eight. Their friendship blossomed when they met again at the funeral and developed into a love that was to stretch across forty years of marriage. As early as sixteen they asked their respective parents to allow them to marry but no blessings were forthcoming. Mary's natural tendency to fly into a temper probably did not increase their chances very much. When they eventually became man and wife, it was the 'quietest of quiet weddings' and they had to pay half-a-crown for two passers-by to act as witnesses.

Their first baby, who was to cause far more than labour pains, arrived in mid-May 1939. And Mary's mother seemed satisfied with her grandchild. It was a boy! She took the infant from Terry and quickly walked from the bedroom making, not cooing noises, but a 'kind of shrill moan'. The sound sent fear surging into Mary. Throughout her child-hood she had heard similar sounds when accompanying her mother on visits to her women friends. They had all made that shrill moan during their funny parties, and by the time of Gary's birth, Mary had come to recognise them for what they were – satanic incantations.

'Go and fetch me my baby!' she yelled at an astonished Terry. He replied with the soothing remarks only to be expected from somebody who had no knowledge of this part of her life. This was only the beginning of the strange influence which her mother began to exert over Gary.

Soon there were other worries to consider, and besides, Gary looked none the worse for those natal incantations. War was declared and the family were evacuated to the Midlands. They had little and sometimes no money, and Mary's mother was far too busy and uninterested to notice, spending her inherited fortune on her lovers. Gary, for whom she appeared to feel something, received her full attention on her rare visits, together with expensive gifts and sweets.

The post-war years brought nagging doubts for Mary, when she was not surrounded by her now four healthy children. She thought of her grandparents, their prayers for her and the sound Christian education they had provided. She had fond memories of walking hand-in-hand with her uncle, a famous preacher, who was to have been her guardian had all her family died prematurely. They had all been staunch Congregationalists, and Mary occasionally felt sad that she had left it all behind in childhood. This was all to change on a pleasant spring day in 1947. She wrote later of what happened.

'I was standing at the sink after lunch with the usual daily mountain of washing at the side. I was not thinking of anything in particular. Suddenly, there stood beside me a very tall figure, six foot six or more, bearded and misty-white in appearance. There was no immediate welcome in my reaction ... I was just overwhelmed with a sense of uncleanness. And then he was gone. My worst feelings were about the bit of a temper I had, and all I can remember was my silent prayer, "Lord, take this away".'

Mary was left with a strange mixture of thoughts. A part of her mind worried about pegging out the washing to make the most of a lovely day. But the front of her mind was occupied with alarming questions. Was she taking leave of her senses? Had she started to see things? And yet it all seemed so real! As the queries deteriorated into doubts, she again resorted to silent prayer. She asked for a sign; some proof to verify her experience.

Before she had finished hanging out the clothes, there was a glorious double rainbow across the sky. She felt as though she was walking on air. The next thing she asked for was a job to do for the Lord.

A few days later Terry's brother asked Mary to act as stand-in pianist for three months at the local Baptist church where he was a member. That job was to last for the following eleven years. As for her new-found peace and joy, they were to be refined in the thousand-and-one ordeals which lay ahead. In retrospect, it seemed that the Lord protected her for the first few days, and then . . .

'About midnight,' recalls Mary, 'Gary started screaming in terror. He came and threw himself on our bed, shaking all over. There was no sleep that night for us, nor for the immediate neighbours, and he continued to scream and cry until about 5 am. Both of us tried to pacify him but it was useless, and he wouldn't tell us what had caused it. It was only much later, in 1981, that he told me what had happened. He said that he was still awake when a black and fearful figure appeared at the foot of his bed. The figure called himself the devil and declared that he had come for Gary's life. It had been given to him, the devil claimed.'

Mary refuses to this day to judge the veracity of Gary's story, in view of his, by then, extensive record of crime and deceit. Only one certain fact remains with her. From that night onwards, Gary was a different person. A seven-year-old lovable imp turned overnight into what can only be described as a 'demon'. The first and most enduring victim of the new Gary was his mother's purse. Next came his three younger sisters whom he began to terrorise – biting, kicking and scratching them. His fellow pupils at school suffered so badly that Mary became a constant visitor to the headmaster's study, and Gary was banned from the play-ground. Neighbours formed queues on occasions as they came to complain of mindless acts of vandalism.

Both Mary and Terry devoted much of their energies, time and love to solving their son's behaviour. On one occasion, they tried to interest him in the piano but that finished within three weeks with two surprises. Gary's teacher came round with both of them. First was the news that the lad had such a natural ear and ability that the teacher felt that he could not teach him anything. The second was the request for payment for the three lessons. Gary had pocketed his piano fees.

The following years of unrelieved deception and destruc-tion were tinged with the happiness of Terry's apparent conversion to Christ and subsequent church work. How-ever, this introduced a new pattern to Gary's war on the world around him. Mary explained . . .

'On the frequent occasions we were engaged in Christian work, we had additional problems with our black lamb. He stole the Sunday school collection. He eavesdropped on church leadership meetings in our home and then made it his business to tell everybody all that we had discussed. The church visitors were intensely embarrassed shortly after we had agreed to have door-to-door visitation for a forth-coming town mission. Gary had beaten them to it, and had demanded contributions for the mission. Of course, he had kept the money.

'It was strange how Gary would often know things he had not been told. We soon took steps to ensure that Gary was otherwise occupied when private matters of the church and home were discussed. Even then, Terry and I used to have arguments when one of us discovered that Gary had knowledge of things that only the two of us knew. The only human explanation was that one of us had said something in an unguarded moment. It was only later, when we compared notes, that we put his source down to something inhuman. The same was true for my mother.'

Looking back to that nightmarish night in the wake of her conversion, Mary can suggest only one explanation. Gary had indeed been consigned to Satan by his grandmother. It was only when Mary became a Christian that the devil came to stake a claim to his own property. But this conclusion was reached only after experiencing the hell that still lay ahead of them.

There were moments of hope, such as the time Gary seemed to settle in the scouts, but they were dashed when he stole the troop's funds. Around the same time, he took his mother's many dancing and music medals, together with his father's accordion, and presented them to the pawnbroker.

With Gary's teens came the police – often! At thirteen he took a car and wrote it off. At fourteen his probation officer suggested he should be sent to borstal, but Gary managed to evade that fate. Terry offered a bike to his son if only he would use the good brain he undoubtedly possessed. Some months later, Gary came top of the class with an average mark of 93%. The following term his average marks were down to 22%.

'Why did you let things go?' his father demanded to know.

'Because you didn't offer me anything!' The lad looked his father straight in the eye as he gave his blunt answer.

Gary would often go missing for hours or stay out overnight. Mary often suspected that he was with his grandmother and involved in her shady activities, though her mother would always deny it. Perhaps, his parents thought, things might change when schooldays finished. Again they were to be disappointed.

Gary's first job ended when he stole the factory tools and pawned them. The second job was a repeat performance. He was sacked from every other job for theft, harassment of female staff or vandalism. The home itself was pillaged often, and by 1957 both Mary and Terry were on the point of collapse after months existing on half-nights of sleep. They had worked out a rota to stand guard on their remaining property, and also to protect their terrified daughters. National Service seemed their last hope.

Gary fancied the uniform of the Coldstream Guards when he arrived at the recruiting office. He was informed that he would have to sign on for an extra year to join the guards, but he told his mother, 'I'll stay as long as I choose. No more, no less!'

The recruiting sergeant noticed Mary's doubtful expression and tried some reassurance.

'Don't worry, ma'am,' he laughed. 'We'll soon lick him into shape.'

The army had stopped laughing within one week of receiving Gary. He had arrived home the weekend after reporting for duty, followed soon afterwards by the military police. They told him in no uncertain terms that he could not take a holiday whenever he felt like it. Seventeen months and several 'holidays' later, he was dishonourably discharged. Meanwhile, a fortune in equipment had gone missing, including his own uniform. The discharging officer called Gary – just nineteen at the time – 'the most evil man he had ever met'.

In the years that followed, Mary's eldest daughter went to Bible college to train for the mission field. Another of the girls went into the nursing profession, while Gary joined the satanists. He opened up various prostitute rings, and later extended his business interests to car thefts, burglary, the drugs market, and practised every 'con-trick' he could dream up. These were mostly aimed at gullible Christians. He seemed to take great delight in taking the church for a ride.

On the family side, he had 'milked' his grandmother dry of all her money before she died. He had caused his father to have a near-fatal heart-attack, and finally, he had used a legal wrangle to cheat his mother out of two properties she inherited on the death of her mother. Mary was left penniless and without any income. When she was rescued by the local authorities and given her present welfare flat, she asked that her address be kept a secret.

Mary wrote her life story as a therapy for herself, and also because she felt it might help others caught up, directly or indirectly, in the occult. It remains unpublished today, save for this truncated and anonymous version, for fear of potentially ruinous legal action. Mary offers many helpful thoughts in her story.

'My life with Gary and my mother and her occult friends has enabled me to pick out the symptoms by which we may recognise those who are involved in the occult. They may be summarised as a revolt against the normal.

Mary set them out as follows, adding to each her own comments.

1. *A radical objection to normal work.* 'Work was undertaken on a whim rather than as a responsible use of time. There was no sense of obligation to society, or even to learn of the necessities of life.'

2. *A taste for extremes* of dress, in colour, shape and style.

3. *An indifference to hygiene of body and environment.* 'At one point when my mother was ill, the district nurse refused to enter her home and treat her, for fear that she would be contaminated and consequently place her other patients in danger.'

4. *A lack of humour and common sense.* 'The women associated with my mother, all spinsters or widows, never smiled and were constantly worried by trivialities. All of their problems could have been solved with a few simple decisions but they seemed to have been robbed of their ability to think straight.'

5. *A contrary pattern of life.* 'Night was preferred to day for whatever was to be done. Cat-naps kept them going. Meals were taken at irregular and unusual times and would be unconventional in content. My mother would often phone up around 5 am when I lived near her, and demand that I come over and cook her dinner. Gary was very similar.'

6. *Death and suicide are favourite topics.* 'There was much fear of dying. The thought of an instant death, chosen in time and manner, seemed to have some minimising effect on that fear. My mother attempted suicide on numerous occasions. Whenever she did, I prayed long and hard for protection for Gary. On every occasion there was a suicide attempt, we would find out that the other had attempted suicide at the identical time, even though they may have been hundreds of miles apart and not seen each other for months. It was as though they were twinned in some satanic fashion.'

7. *An anxious atmosphere.* 'Their presence militated against a relaxed and restful environment. Their company seemed to drain me and send me into a state of nervous exhaustion after even a short while. Was this the opposing spiritual force at work?'

8. *Lethargy.* 'Despite the restlessness, there was usually a slow, lazy habit of mind. (Gary was the only exception I knew to this rule, and then only when he was up to no good).'

9. *A belief in man's goodness.* 'This may have been largely absent from their own lives, but it was the prevailing view of human nature. Man was really quite a good species, they believed. This was especially true of my mother's view of Gary, and vice versa.'

10. *A reversal of the biblical.* 'Each of the above is a contradiction of God's Word. It hardly needs to be said that there is also a total rejection of moral principles. Ethics were abandoned and despised in areas concerning sex, other people's property, personal lifestyles, care of young or old, and law and order.'

11. *Spiritual deceit.* 'In the last hours of her life, my mother seemed to turn to the Lord. I still pray that this is true. But Gary made innumerable professions of faith from childhood onwards. The most significant was in the middle of a prison riot when Gary had joined the roof-top protestors to escape the violence of psychopaths who were systematically tearing the prison apart inside. Later, as a 'Christian evangelist', Gary would speak of meeting God in the hours of comparative tranquillity on the prison roof. Just before his release from this five-year sentence, he sent a threatening letter to Terry saying that he intended to 'get him'. Terry died as a result of his injuries in a car crash just hours before Gary was released.

Soon afterwards, Gary was back on drugs, living with a girl, and then came numerous confidence tricks. We are not called upon to judge each other. I can only point out the immoral lifestyle that accompanied his profession and the evidence of spiritual deceit. I leave the rest to God.'

12. *A lack of love.* 'A person involved in the occult is totally preoccupied with himself and his own desires. Whether they are actually his desires, or those of the devil, must remain speculation. Certainly, they do try to escape the desires via suicide on occasions.

'I have learned that the love Christ gives to us is a mighty power. I am left to live out my life with only the few possessions I have managed to buy from my pension, because of Gary. But I love him. And it is only the love of Christ in me that enables me to say that. It is, in fact, solely the all-powerful love of God, expressed through each one of us, that will save people lost in the occult. I still pray for Gary and continue to hope that he will eventually live up to the professions of faith that he has made. I pray that God will really meet with him this time in prison. How much of his life he is personally responsible for, and how much his grandmother's incantations affected him, I do not know. It would be a dangerous practice to absolve those affected by Satan, even Gary. Again, we must leave this with the Lord.'

*   *   *

We need to remember that Mary's twelve 'revolts from the normal' relate only to those in satanism and lower forms of witchcraft. The majority in other occult areas are no different in outward appearance from the normal person in the street. Many hold down regular jobs and quite a few are highly-paid, professional people. Many witches with whom I have discussed Christianity have a real sense of humour and pleasant personalities. Some are charming and a delight to converse with. On a personal level, I find this the most distressing. As a mere imperfect mortal, I find myself working twice as hard to introduce those whom I like to the Lord. This includes more than a few in the occult. I want them to share the Person who has filled my life with such abundance.

It is important to remember that the satanism highlighted in this chapter is exceptional. Most in the occult would be at home in your local golf club. You could even introduce them to your church's women's guild and they would not look out of place. Ostensibly the average occultist is a perfectly normal person.

9
New Age for Old

The potential of the New Age Movement is frightening. It could even now be starting the greatest revolution our British culture has ever known. It has already changed the pattern of life in America, and it seems as though our turn has now arrived. Christians need to be ready for it, and the most alarming aspect is that the vast majority have never heard of it.

The last time I preached on the New Age before writing this chapter, I asked for a show of hands from those who had heard of it. Two hands showed in the two hundred–strong congregation. After mentioning some of the New Age practices and beliefs, I asked again for a show of hands from those who knew friends and neighbours who were involved. This time virtually everybody raised a hand. We meet the New Age and are influenced by it in everyday life, yet few Christians understand its full impact.

What are we to make of this movement?

Some commentators' views

Is it 'an unparalleled mystical conspiracy threatening today's world,' as Caryl Matrisciana maintains in her book *Gods of the New Age*?[1] Hal Lindsay states that 'the West has been invaded by the East' and 'every Christian must be equipped to meet the onslaught of Eastern thought'.

Christian attorney Constance Cumbey goes a step further in *The Hidden Dangers of the Rainbow* when she writes of the 'coming age of barbarism', and describes the New Agers as a 'viable movement that truly meets the scriptural requirements for the Antichrist and the political movement that will bring him on the world scene'.[2]

Are the Americans going over the top again, or is this an indictment which we should place on trial? At least one Englishman thinks so. He is Roy Livesey, a leading New Age watcher on this side of the Atlantic. For him, understanding the New Age is to witness the 'preparations for Antichrist's One World Government'. His books include 'an exposé of Satan's secret rulers on earth' and a strong 'plea for discernment in the Church'.[3]

Perhaps, with typical English reserve, we should go along with Alice and Stephen Lawhead's *Pilgrim's Guide to the New Age* (Lion Publishing). This lavish book provides us with a full-colour holiday brochure; a 'sightseer's guide for anyone journeying through this brave new world'.[4] The Lawheads may be American, but they have produced a book which comfortably suits the English mood of tolerance. It has a 'once upon a time' approach and, while avoiding negative criticisms of New Age philosophies, it takes the reader on a tour of some of the more positive Christian beliefs.

Secular books on the New Age tend to treat it as the latest fad; the 'in thing' of the eighties, full of Alternative Types and quaint ideas about the 'good life' down on the organic, backyard farm. In a style guide to the New Age called *Spilling the Beans*, Martin Stott informs us that 'perhaps as much as 10% of the adult population' in Britain are New Agers.[5] They are likely to be found breast-feeding in the high street while swopping telephone numbers of their family acupuncturists. They then hop into an old Morris Minor or CV6 and drive home to the 'muesli belt'.

Are New Agers just simply home-grown nature-lovers, or are they one of the greatest dangers to confront Christendom? You will have to make your own judgement as we investigate. Two things, however, are certain.

Firstly, the New Age is sweeping through the American culture with the speed of a giant hogweed. If the normal pattern is followed, Britain will experience an even greater invasion in the next decade.

Secondly, the New Age is 'into' the occult in a big way. It is the new paganism, or rather the old variety with a facelift and a fresh application of make-up. In short, no book which sets out to analyse modern occultism can afford to avoid this new movement.

What is the New Age?

It defies a one-sentence description. It is all things to all men ... and this is perhaps its number one axiom. Whatever 'turns you on' is okay, so long as it is not connected with modern materialism or the one-God religions, like Christianity, Judaism or Islam.

The New Age is not one vast organisation. It is more a movement involving tens of thousands of associated sub-groups, all of which are independent, though sympathetic to each other. Several groups claim to exert their influence, but insist that it is no more than that. In the absence of any organisational identity, the best way to describe New Agers is to catalogue the creed common to most.

1. *They believe in self-realisation.* The first commandment is to love your self with all your mind, with all your soul, with all your heart and with all your strength. No New Ager would put it this way. They would far rather think of it as realising their strengths and weaknesses. 'Removing the plank from one's own eye,' was how one explained it. The overwhelming tendency, though, is to so concentrate on 'self' that others are excluded. The New Ager's prime goal is

to reach into himself, to plumb the depths of his psyche and live in harmony with the universal force. He is called to the realisation that he is part of the force, the force is god, and therefore he is god. His first duty is to realise his full potential as a human being, and to explore all possibilities until he reaches enlightened fulfilment.

So far, the New Age is about as new as man himself. Adam and Eve were successfully tempted to become 'like God'. That was Satan's first ploy (Genesis 3:5). Eastern religions – some of them the oldest known to man – have taught people for millennia to find their gods within themselves.

2. *They believe that all is one.* Essentially, there is no difference between you and the rose bush in your front garden. Your pet goldfish and you are basically two 'expressions' of the one, cosmic force. In fact, the gurus of the East teach that the goldfish might well have been your great, great grandmother in a previous existence if she did not make the grade as a human being. In the West, reincarnation is 'packaged' in more attractive terms, with the talents and gifts of each life being passed on to succeeding lives. This 'snowballing' effect is what evolution is all about, they claim. It is big business in New Age circles (see Chapter 14).

All that we can see, feel, touch, taste and hear is of one, all-pervading force – the god force. If god is in everything, then why not worship everything? New Agers generally think that this is a good idea. Mother Earth must be served, hence the explosion in ecology groups and Green Parties in the last few years. And what about those dogs and monkeys being used for experimental purposes? How dare we treat our 'brothers and sisters' in such a cruel fashion! Animals, in essence, are viewed as of equal value to humans, so the Animal Liberation Front sees no great difficulty in maiming humans to free animals.

Again, we find nothing new. Seeing God in everything

has been known for nearly 400 years as pantheism, though the idea is as old as religion itself. This teaches that the whole universe is identified with 'God' or 'nature' – you choose which to call it. The idea, however, has been in existence for as long as man has worshipped. In Hinduism, practically everything is the manifestation of a god, and even the most seasoned guru has difficulty in keeping track of all of them. Hindus know the cosmic energy as the kundalini or serpent force, and this is said to be coiled around the base of the spine in every human being. Pantheism is also present in Buddhism, with Brahman being the life-force.

Pantheism conflicts with the Christian view of the fundamental distinction between God and that which he has created (Hebrews 11:3). Christianity also teaches that man is a special creation, related but distinct from the animals, made in God's image and likeness (Genesis 1:26–27).

It has to be stressed that Christianity also takes seriously the welfare of planet earth and its animals. Ecology and protection of animals from cruelty is part of man's God-given role as stewards of the earth (Genesis 1:28). New Agers claim that Christians have abdicated from ruling the planet in a life-sustaining way. They have taken over the Christian's own cliché and complain that many are 'too heavenly-minded to be any earthly use!' In some areas, Christians may have no alternative but to plead guilty to this charge. As the question goes: 'What on earth are we doing for heaven's sake?'

3. *May the force be with us.* To achieve self-realisation, and to get in tune with the cosmic force, the New Agers are introduced to the oldest techniques known to pagan man. These include yoga and meditation, hypnosis, gurus, I Ching (the Chinese divination technique), and astrology. Some of these are used to bring about an 'altered state of consciousness' in which reality can be perceived in different ways, not unlike our chaos magician who throws himself into his 'void'. The force within can also be manipulated through . . .

Dieting, in which you are discouraged from eating meat because it provokes unhelpful vibrations and produces what might be called static interference in meditation. This is said to block the way to true communion with the spiritual force.

Jogging, and the whole keep-fit scene, can be exploited to put you in touch with the force. One woman athlete said, 'Running is better than sex!' This could refer to the New Age spiritual 'high' that some athletes attain through exercise. I say 'could', because running and hard exercise can do wonders for body, mind and spirit without any New Age-type influence. However, the latest approach to the force is through hyperventilation (special patterns of breathing) and the chanting of yoga mantras synchronised with the jogging rhythm. Both these can produce trance-like vacuums allowing, it is claimed, the participant to reach pure spiritual union with the force.

Other techniques used to foster harmony with the force and improve mindpower include bioenergetics, Sufi dancing, biofeedback, positive thinking programmes, Silva Mind Control, martial arts, and the use of isolation tanks.

Christians beware! At this point, Christians need to protect themselves against over–reaction. We certainly need to be wary of yoga, Transcendental Meditation, hypnosis, and astrology and we shall come to these later. However, the Christian has every right to keep himself fit and healthy. It is good to observe a correct diet, even if for some it means being a vegetarian. Breathing exercises can certainly be helpful and the average athlete or singer would be somewhat limited without the control that such exercises bring. The body is, after all, the temple of the Holy Spirit (1 Corinthians 3:16), and as such should be maintained properly. It is not, however, to be regarded as a receptacle to be emptied and purified for an infilling of some cosmic force.

Origins of the New Age

Here again, the question has no single-sentence answer. We have to investigate several paths.

1. *Eastern origins*

I have already hinted that the New Age is a revamp of ancient and still existing practices mainly from India, Tibet and China. It is the Eastern religions repackaged and made presentable for consumption by Western minds.

It does seem amazing that the West should now be entertaining an Eastern worldview which has created such cruelty and agonising poverty across a massive portion of the globe. Much of the poverty, chaos and disease of the East can be directly attributed to its religious beliefs and ideologies. The wealth of the West has been accomplished largely through applying the beliefs of Christianity to everyday life. It was the Judaeo-Christian work ethic which produced an Industrial Revolution and brought modern technology to the West. It was the Christian stress on man's free will that enabled the individual to realise that he had a choice. He did not have a karma; he was not locked on to an inescapable railway line to a predetermined destiny – an idea that has frozen the will of millions in the East. Modern science could only have come from a belief that there was a God who had made all things to a certain design.[6] The father of modern science, Isaac Newton, was as much at home in the pews receiving blessings from above, as in the orchard wondering why apples kept falling on his head. It was a belief in a designing and orderly God which made it possible for him to think there might be a consistent cause for his 'headaches'.

To be sure, the modern West has turned into a corrupt and greedy Scrooge, with each affluent nation ever-reluctant to share its gross national product with a starving and emaciated Third World. The First World's miserly materialism is enough to make any honest seeker yearn for a new alternative or age. Our Western pre-occupation with concrete, plastic, silicon chips and nuclear bombs is causing increasing numbers to retreat to the simple life of nature. I therefore have some sympathy with the New Ager, but I cannot understand why he is in such a hurry to rebuild his world on foundational beliefs which have already crippled millions upon millions of fellow human beings. It seems far more reasonable to accept the great progress that Christian thinking has brought, while understanding the equally valid Christian teaching that man is a wretched sinner and needs to be changed. The Christian beliefs work for the good of man. The corruptions in the West have come from man's failure to apply those beliefs correctly. The Eastern philosophies and religions have little to offer in improving the lot of mankind.

2. *Western beginnings*

There have always been the eccentrics and academics who have travelled the East only to return home to announce great spiritual discoveries. One who was taken seriously was Madame Helena Petrovna Blavatsky, who founded the Theosophical Society in 1875, a much-quoted doyen of occult magic today. Her society declared that the twin enemies were Christianity and science and 'both must be made to respect their Indian betters'. Several publications came from the society, including *Isis Unveiled* and *The Secret Doctrine*, both produced in a trance state and automatically written under the guidance of the 'Masters'. These 'Masters' were said to be the hidden wise men who were spread around the world with the aim of bringing in a New World Order.

Rector's wife Alice Ann Bailey and an outrageous accomplice called Annie Besant continued laying the foundations of a New Age Movement, both being governed by the 'Masters'. Their books were heavily influenced by psychic and occultic philosophies. A publishing company named Lucifer[7] was established in 1922, which distributed the writings to an increasing network of New Age groups. The goals were to establish a New World Order which would prepare the way for the New World 'messiah', the Lord Maitreya. They also aimed for the elimination of dogmatic religions, such as Christianity, and the establishment of a one-world government and religion. A New World Order would include a universal credit card system,[8] the use of the figures '666' (the mark of the beast in Revelation 13:18), and an all-planet food authority and tax system. The modern-day New Age Movement seems to get most of its direction from the Findhorn Foundation in Scotland, though Findhorn would insist that there is no leadership, only a loose confederation of groups 'doing their own thing'. The thousands of groups and organisations are as diverse as the colours of the rainbow, and they have taken this natural phenomenon as the New Age symbol.

This is the information which Constance Cumbey finds alarming in her book, *Hidden Dangers of the Rainbow*. She maintains that many well-meaning New Agers are innocently misled through hypnosis and mind-control and are unaware of the movement's ultimate goals. They are more victims than villains.

Miss Cumbey's work is a prophetic book and, as with all prophecy, the test of it lies in the future. Is her prophecy coming true? Will this really be the movement which introduces the Antichrist to the world?

Personally, I will wait and see. As an over-zealous convert from Roman Catholicism, I have identified my fair share of Antichrists in the past – all centred on Rome and the Pope. Some of my theories have fallen to pieces, including the nine-nation European Common Market being the ten-horned beast, with the Vatican, of course, being the tenth state. When other nations subsequently joined the EEC, I decided it was time to hold fire on future Antichrist prophecies.

However, a watchful eye needs to be kept on the New

Age phenomena. I notice, for instance, the growing number of families in my own area who are involved in Eastern mysticism and the soft fringes of the occult. When I visit my home city of Manchester, or travel to London, New Age-types seem to greet me in every other conversation. I note the results of two extensive local surveys we conducted into beliefs. One of the questions asked, 'What do you believe happens to you after death?' In the adult survey, 11% opted for reincarnation. When it came to the youth survey, an incredible 23% claimed a belief in reincarnation, which is only 2% lower than a nationwide opinion poll in America.

The findings of my own investigations into New Age groups and publications are also noteworthy. The following four seem to be typical:

New Life Designs organises festivals of mind, body and spirit, and is celebrating its tenth anniversary at the time of writing. The festivals are demonstrations of Eastern and occult practices, and they promote a 'Networking Game' throughout the UK. It is described as a 'method of meeting, and exchanging meaningful information, with like-minded individuals and groups'. The founder-director, Graham Wilson, explains in the group's anniversary leaflet:

> This networking of previously lone individuals and groups will be highlighted through a number of networking facilities including the innovative Networking Game. I believe we truly have something to celebrate, not only what has been achieved but what must now be possible in the coming decade.[9]

The Wrekin Trust runs courses on astrology and psychology, the way of the Kabbalah (their spelling), psychic sensitivity and others of a similar nature in many parts of the country. The trust was founded by Sir George Trevelyan[10] in 1971 and seeks to promote 'awareness and study of the spiritual nature of man and the universe'. It 'does not offer any one way to the truth but helps people find the disciplines most suited to them'. It promotes the workshops of Ruth White, 'a practising sensitive counsellor and healer' who 'established a strong and ongoing contact with her guide and communicator Gildas over twenty years ago'.

Malcolm Lazarus, co–director with Sir George of the Trust, was converted to the 'Wrekin' philosophy when he experienced a release of 'kundalini' energy. Mr Lazarus described it 'as if a bolt of energy shot up my spine and burst through the top of my head. I walked around flaming like a Roman candle.'[11]

The New Humanity Journal is published internationally bi–monthly. It 'speaks for the new concepts required to create a better world structure', and works 'towards a spiritually–based civilisation'. The journal aims 'for peace, non–confrontation, unity in diversity, mental liberation and harmony with the Godhead'. One article in the June–July 1984 edition equates God with Brahman and Buddha, and it advertises 'Merlin', the new magic to put us in touch with the new energy. The journal also publishes what might be called The Ten Commandments of New Humanity, though the magazine invites its readers to 'make up their own' if they prefer. The first commandment is 'Thou shalt remember that the Essence and We are One and should strive towards that proper integration.'[12]

The Aetherius Society is probably the leading light in the New Age Movement in this country, and has a growing membership under the guidance of His Eminence, Sir George King OSG, PhD, D Litt. The knighthood is of foreign origin bestowed by the Constantinian Order of St George in Italy. The letters after his name are from the Independent Theological Seminary in Nuyf, California. This is part of the International Evangelists Crusade, which is legally authorised to ordain ministers.

The society claims that there are 'cosmic masters' in the universe and that they have come 'to give priceless teachings to man to help him prepare for the New World and to bring a great millennium of peace'. Jesus and other religious leaders came from them, it is claimed, and there is now a spiritual hierarchy on our planet known as the Great White Brotherhood (white in this case refers to 'white magic').

When Dr Richard Lawrence, the society's secretary, learned that I was writing a Christian appraisal of paganism and the occult, he pointed out that Aetherius' members fully revered Jesus, and were convinced of his virgin birth and resurrection. Dr Lawrence, who was confirmed by one of the previous archbishops in Canterbury Cathedral, said that his society would never allow one of their leaders to undermine these essential doctrines as had happened in the Church of England.

The 'Masters', said Dr Lawrence, were responsible for the miraculous birth and resurrection of Jesus! These 'Masters' were at present in a spacecraft orbiting earth and their power was being magnified three thousand times by an international network of groups using Christian prayer and Buddhist mantras. He believed that these groups were helping to alleviate the effects of catastrophies caused by the dawning of the New Age.

'All phases of our mission are helping to alleviate things such as earthquakes and hurricanes,' he explained. 'In the recent hurricanes in the south of England [October 1987], fifteen people lost their lives. This was sad, but we believe that the figure could have been nearer 1,500.'

We wait for time to test Constance Cumbey's prophecy that the New Age is the herald of the Antichrist. I have to recognise that my own findings in no way rule out the possibility.

3. *The Age of Aquarius*

Astrology provides another origin for the New Age. It is perhaps best known through the smash-hit sixties musical

Hair! Its lyrics and tunes celebrated the dawning of the 'Age of Aquarius' and had the whole nation chanting 'Hare Krishna' for months.

For many it was their first introduction to a New Age in which the governments and countries would fall or be changed, society and the family would expire and a new order would rise up out of the ashes of old values and beliefs.

Underlying the musical and, indeed the whole New Age Movement, are the astrological ages of man – each age lasting about two thousand years. Adam is said to have been the herald of the Taurian Age (the age of the bull which gives life), while Abraham began the Age of Aries (sacrificing the ram instead of his son). Jesus Christ brought in the Piscean Age (hence, it is alleged, the ichthus fish sign of the new church and the numerous allusions to fishermen being turned into fishers of men). As we approach the close of the next two thousand years, we are told to look forward to a new age – the Age of Aquarius, the water carrier. This is the age of service, sharing, loving and caring and the age when man must also be prepared to help himself. There is also the thought that we are inheritors of the previous three ages and that we become all that they have been. The first age was said to belong to God the Father, the second to God the Son, and the last age to God the Spirit. Now it is the age of fulfilled man who takes in all the Trinity and becomes one with them. All we need to do now, we are told, is to wake up to the fact that we are God. Salvation is found by reaching this enlightenment, and enables the editor of *The New Humanity* to write, 'It is no longer a question of "What do we do to be saved?" but more a realisation of "How do we express a richer, more abundant lifestyle as saved individuals?"'[13]

The true Aquarian is said to be friendly, progressive, creative, inventive, independent, original, tolerant, refined, artistic, discreet, optimistic and fond of science and lite-rature. The New Ager certainly demonstrates some of these qualities in the way that he creates and refines an original artistic fiction. It often seems that the New Ager has invented his 'science' independently of any authority except the optimistic inner influences, and that of lumps of matter whizzing through space.

4. *The happy hippie origins*

The Californian sun shines on some strange, off-beat groups but the vast majority are eclipsed by newer and crazier fads. The hippies have proved a sturdier breed than most. They became a worldwide phenomenon and are still in circulation. They traditionally surface on British television every summer solstice as they trek across country to join the druids at Stonehenge, much to the dismay of local farmers and the police.

The hippies were a sixties reaction to a world of materialism. It was a time for flower power and a return to nature and the simple ways. It was a sixties of the Beatles and their guru, Maharishi Yogi, and the new search for spirituality in Eastern meditation, drugs and psychedelia. It was a disillusioned generation which went east to find the new answers.

We realise today that this reactionary generation grew up to be the most materialistic the world has ever known. Many of the drop-outs eventually left their flowers, cut their hair and dropped back in to the 'rat race' of business, commerce and industry. The old rebellion was squeezed out by the pressure of survival, and the 'young ones' conformed to create a new world, not out of spiritual charity, but out of silicon chips.

It is now also dawning on us that, while they may have dropped their hippie beads and trinkets, they failed to let go of their new world view. Our modern Western world is consequently run by captains of industry, commerce and business who have an underlying Eastern philosophy. In America, those guru-led hippie students are now in their fifties and the New Age is part of the shopfloor and even in the curriculum in university and school.

Britain, of course, lagged behind the States, but it is now beginning to surface. In Skelmersdale New Town in Lancashire, for instance, a large Transcendental Meditation village was under construction at the time of writing to house the workers on an already existing TM industrial estate. (More about this when we look at TM.)

Now we look more closely at the techniques which are being used to put Western New Age man in touch with nature and its 'force'.

10

'Stageprops' of the Occult

Robert, a man in his late twenties with a long history of occult involvement, grew up in what he now knows to be one of the most haunted farmhouses in Lancashire on the Fylde coast. One morning in his childhood he came downstairs, opened a door 'and it was like below the decks of an old galleon complete with hammocks hanging up'. Robert explained that this was not unusual.

'I used to see and feel things in the house, but being a child I just took it for granted that everybody else was seeing and feeling the same things. This is how my interest started. Later on, I learned about tarot cards and ouija boards and just drifted into using these props, because they made it easier to see and feel these things.'

Here we get the first hint of why those in the occult and the New Age of paganism use special techniques and paraphernalia. Talk to any magician or occultist for long enough, and the word 'props', or something similar, will crop up. Jim, a converted satanist from the London area, spoke of the time he was being groomed for initiation. 'They taught us how to use all the divination equipment . . . . I had a particular gift with the tarot cards . . . not using the traditional interpretations which are given on the back of any £5-pack from W H Smiths. Each card is used as an aid. You deal a card, study it, meditate on it, let your mind go blank and allow a picture to come into your mind.'

A professional clairvoyant in Preston told me, 'You know what a card is supposed to stand for. Or you can look at the star chart cast at somebody's birthdate. But the secret is to read between the cards or astrological signs. Whatever I use, whether it is a crystal ball, a pack of cards, or an article belonging to somebody, it is simply a stageprop; something that gives me the right vibrations and helps me to see the right pictures.'

Most in the occult agree that the paraphernalia they use are simply aids in contacting and manipulating the power. This is a vital point to grasp. Christians can waste hours trying to explain the illogicality of, for instance, astrological predictions. The fortune-teller will probably agree with the problems, and then tell you how irrelevant they are. The star systems, right or wrong, are only there to provide the right atmosphere; to set the mood; to spark off communion with the spirit or energy force.

We do, however, need to spend time looking at some of the shortcomings of the 'props'. That next-door neighbour dabbler you are so concerned about is much more likely to be involved in the 'soft-occult', and may still be open to a little reasoning. It is true that we live in an age when people are increasingly more likely to act on intuition, but many are still able to calculate when two and two add up to five. On that basis, we shall survey some of these New Age and occult forms of divination.

Astrology

This is a belief that celestial bodies in some way influence our planet and ourselves (the macrocosm affecting the micro-cosm). It goes back to the days when people used to worship heavenly bodies as gods. Astrology reached its 'modern' form around AD 140 under the guidance of Ptolemy, the famous Greek astronomer. He, of course, assumed that the earth was the hub of the universe, and also that the cosmos was controlled by celestial beings, rather like the living beings or cherubim of Ezekiel. He placed the beings, pictured as animals, in a belt embracing the known universe, and divided it into the twelve equal houses of the zodiac (Aries, Taurus, Gemini, Cancer, Leo, Virgo, Libra, Sagittarius, Scorpio, Capricorn, Aquarius and Pisces). These houses were allocated a month each in a given year. Each of the known bodies at that time – the sun, Saturn, Jupiter, Mars, Venus, Mercury and the moon – were said to have powers or characteristic influences.

Popular Natal Astrology assumes that you can assess a person's strengths and weaknesses by charting the sky at his exact moment of birth. You do this by assessing which of the 'stars' and their characteristics dominate his house at birth. This is supposed to paint a picture of his personality, and the astrologer can then go on to tell the person his future by a complicated process of advancing the stars.

Christianity in the early days had little effect on the popularity of astrology. But Copernicus dealt it a crippling blow when he discovered that the sun, and not the earth, was the centre of our insignificant system. The rationalism of the eighteenth century, together with the discovery of two more planets (Uranus in 1781 and Neptune in 1839) eventually relegated astrology to the absurd. It was not until just before the turn of the present century that it was revived by those who sought to promote the occult and a New Age mentality. The Theosophical Society and Madame Blavatsky, with her mediumistic relationships with 'The Masters', led the way.

How it managed to survive in our sophisticated century remains one of the modern wonders of the world. The science of astronomy had by this time totally undermined the old Ptolemaic system. Now that we understand that the axis of the earth has moved significantly, we realize that today's stargazers see a different sky from their predecessors. Added to this came the discovery of yet another planet – Pluto – in 1932.

What is even more remarkable against this background is that modern science has now not only taken an interest in the mystical art of the Zodiac, but is actually trying to prove that a person's stars do have an effect. Several doctors, professors and scientists came together in London in November 1987 to compare notes on current research. A professor from Manchester presented his analysis of criminals' birth dates, which showed that a higher number than average were born in summer. Of course, it could simply mean that winter foetuses might not get the same diet as others. Journalist Diana Hutchinson, of the *Daily Mail*, pointed out that it might be a question of 'the young baby left alone while the parents went out to play in the summer sunshine'. It could also be, dare I state it, a case of criminals enjoying a more active sex life in the long winter nights.

There was also the French psychologist Michel Gauguelin, who has shown an inconclusive link between a child's birth date and a future career. He has also shown that a child is likely to share the same birth months as other relatives. But perhaps this not so much to do with 'stars' as the fact that related people often share the same preferences when planning their families.

The scientists, incidentally, had no help from the nation's leading astrologers, such as Derek and Julia Parker, Jillie Collings, Russell Grant and Patric Walker. They avoided the conference as did the Faculty of Astrological Studies which trains two hundred and fifty astrologers a year. The only assistance for the scientists were from the Astrological Association of Great Britain who organised it.

Diana Hutchinson, in her article, cited the astrologers' resentful reactions.[1]

Patric Walker: 'Astrology is an art and always will be. The thing that disturbs me about statistics is that they can be interpreted to mean anything. The thing that worries me about scientists is that they say one thing one day – like cholesterol is bad for you – and another thing the next day.'

Jillie Collings: 'I frankly don't care what these scientists are out to prove. It would be the same as me going to a medical conference or to the stock exchange and telling them where they were going wrong. I just remember the scientist who told the Wright brothers their machine would never fly.'

Student astrologers, along with some scientists, often try to defend astrology as a logical workable system, but the old hands know better than to try. They know that their charts and signs are merely 'props' to aid their art.

Another problem for the astrologer is the widely varying lifestyles and fortunes of people who are born at identical times and places. There is a case to argue for twins, though genetic similarities have more to do with their parallel lives than do the stars. But what about babies born in the same city at the same time? My wife still knows a person born shortly after her at the same maternity hospital. They are psychologically, spiritually and in personality as different as chalk and cheese. This would not be the case if astrology worked. A nine-year-old boy has become the youngest in history to pass an A-level in mathematics at the time of writing. But why should he alone make the headlines? Why was there only one maths genius out of all the children born in his part of the country on the same day? As other critics of astrology have asked: why is there only one William Shakespeare?

The only thing that can be said for astrology is that it makes money for those who write and publish horoscopes, despite being wrong on most occasions. British newspapers collated all predictions concerning the course and outcome of the last war. The vast majority failed to materialise. Astrologers (not including medium Jeanne Dixon) were predicting re-election for President John F Kennedy right up to the time of his assassination. German war records rescued after

the last war showed that Hitler's use of astrology was one of
the major causes for his demise. Almanacs rarely forecast
the future accurately. If an almanac editor gets ten per cent
of his predictions right in a given year, he counts it a
success.

If astrology was limited to the latest fad of providing
newspaper horoscopes for the family's 'pampered pooch', it
would be comical.[2] The Aquarian alsation or the Capricorn
collie would come to little harm from canine astrology.
However, when it comes to their owners, it can be a sad and
destructive business. People hooked on horoscopes sometimes refuse to try for good jobs because the signs are against
them. Some people feel restricted in their choices or limited
to their present station in life, because their birthcharts
declare that they are unlikely to better themselves. Then
there are the men and women who give up trying to
strengthen their weak areas because they are informed that
the conjunction of the planets at the time of their births will
not allow them to do so. There are even the odd cases of
women who refuse to get out of bed until their husbands
have brought up their morning paper horoscopes! There is
growing evidence of young people getting bored with their
daily stars and seeking greater thrills in darker occult areas. I
have come to believe that the soft occult more often than not
leads to the hard stuff. Certainly it is a sad form of bondage.

The biggest problem with astrology is that it stops people
from worshipping the one true God. They are too busy
worshipping balls of dead matter wandering through space.
The Bible has more than a few things to say about astrology
and fortune-telling.

> Let your astrologers come forward,
> those stargazers who make predictions
> month by month.
> Let them save you from what is
> coming upon you.

> Surely they are like stubble;
> the fire will burn them up.
> They cannot save themselves
> from the power of the flame.
> (Isaiah 47:13–14)

Other biblical renunciations are in Deuteronomy 18:10,11; 1 Samuel 28:3; 2 Kings 21:6 and 23:24; Isaiah 8:19,20; and Daniel 2:2. The Lord clearly despises the practice of reaching for the stars instead of turning to him.

One final question needs to be dealt with before leaving astrology. This chapter suggests that the stars are merely a 'stageprop' for contacting the cosmic force, which the Bible describes as an evil spirit. The question must be this: Why does the devil not allow his 'prophets' to be right all the time? I believe there are four answers to this:

1. The Bible makes it clear that the devil and his forces are the masters of misrepresentation. They delight to lead human beings astray (Matthew 24:24; John 8:44). This is not a self-defeating strategy, as some occultists may claim. The devil is careful to dangle just as much as is needed to keep occultists interested.

2. The devil is limited in his knowledge of the future. He does not have God's ability to know and see all.

3. There are many frauds and tricksters in this area. One editor, for instance, got away with reprinting old horoscopes for four weeks before a reader eventually rang to complain.

4. It is a spiritual principle that we will receive only as much as we are prepared to use. Jesus makes this clear in the parable of the ten minas (Luke 19:11f). The devil can only 'ape' these principles. Those who only 'play' at astrology are protected to a certain degree by their own reluctance to give themselves fully to it. True, they are playing with great danger, but they may never really experience communion with the evil force behind astrology. For them it is simply a party game or a hobby. The same could be said for

Christianity. There are so many in our pews who play at worship; who go to church but never truly open themselves up to power of God's Spirit.

Those who play at the stars will never reach them. Those who give much, to them will much be returned. Could this possibly be the truth surrounding one Michel de Nostredame? Nostradamus published his *Centuries* in 1555 and they have never been out of print since. He is said to have prophesied the French Revolution, the Crimean War, two devastating world wars, the rise and fall of Hitler, and the rise and rise of the Arab wealth. He has been so accurate, some claim, that they have dubbed him the 'historian of the future'. Nostradamus apparently forecast a soviet invasion of Britain in the next decade, the fall of the Houses of Parliament and a nuclear wipe-out at the turn of the millennium.

Nostradamus, astrologer supreme and ritual magician, set out his prophecies in coded four-line stanzas with sometimes appalling alternative rhymes. Some have called him a drunkard and assume that he saw puce poetry instead of pink elephants. Many more have claimed him to be a genius of the hidden writings of the past; an unsurpassed esoteric; an extraordinary magician who deliberately mixed up his mysterious verses to hide them from weaklings and meddlars.

His writings are notoriously difficult to interpret and understand. But even this cannot hide an inexplicable accuracy.

Perhaps Nostradamus epitomised the spiritual principle: to him who has and employs, will more and more be given. Which spirit was responsible for inspiring his prophecies we shall look at in Chapter 13.

Palm reading

Palmistry, as practised in seaside booths and council-house sitting rooms, is the study of the human hand to assess the characteristics and future of its owner. Assemble a handful of palm-readers in one room, and you will end up with an argument. It often seems that there are as many ways of reading hands as there are palmists. One concentrates solely on hand lines (chiromancy) while others are only interested in the form of the hand (chirognomy). One palm reader may deduce her findings from a comparison between lines and hand form, while another may simply use the palm rather as she uses, at other times, a crystal ball. In this case, the hand is simply an autoscope – a 'stageprop' – used to help a medium contact her familiar spirit.

Fussing over vertical life-lines, pondering horizontal heart and head lines and anxiously measuring the girdle of Venus and zone of intuition, seems a desperate and futile way to fill the aching emptiness in many a woman's life.

It seemed especially desperate at a charter fair in my home town as we watched a local housewife who had set up her fortune-telling tent. Admittance was gained by crossing *her* palm with a £1 coin. Throughout the day-long fair, there was never less than a queue of about a dozen. Four hours after the fair had officially closed, there were still six women waiting to have their palms read.

Kurt Koch tells the story of a thirteen-year-old girl who was told by a palmist that she would die in her thirtieth year. The girl threw caution to the wind and tried to make the most of every minute via sex, drink, numerous abortions, and late-night revels. She died of ulcerated colitis at twenty-four.[3] More happily, a colleague told me of a seventeen-year-old girl in his last parish who was cruelly told that she would be dead in a year. She is now a teacher, a mother of two lovely children, and well into her thirties.

The sad truth and emptiness of palmistry can be seen in the hand lines of many elderly, but still lively, people today. According to their lines, they should have died thirty or forty years ago!

Card laying

Cartomancy involves divining the future by reading cards. A normal pack of playing cards can be used but the most popular version is tarot. In the first version, each card laid represents a value, such as love or luck. With 52 cards to turn up, the combinations are practically inexhaustible.

Tarot is even more complex with 78 cards, 22 of which are decorated with highly-symbolic pictures with names like The Hanging Man, the Pope, the Devil, the Lovers, Judgement, and an untitled image of death. These cards are called *atouts* or the Major Arcana. The remaining 56 are the Minor Arcana, and are similar to ordinary playing cards. Most clairvoyants restrict themselves to the pictures for divination. They also readily acknowledge that the symbols are not as important as the impressions, imaginings and emotions they provoke. They are simply 'props' to aid divination. Some claimed that the powers which they tapped were either from God or from their own subconscious mind. Others believed it was some unknown, but benevolent, cosmic force.

Jim, the ex-satanist we met earlier in this chapter, does not mince his words. He agrees that tarot are the 'devil's picture cards' and speaks of the time he was robbed of his powers just before his conversion.

'I lived in a large house converted into flats. At the time I was training ... to cross the abyss or pit to become an Adept. It was a dangerous time, and what made it even more dangerous was the arrival of some strange new neighbours. I suddenly found that I was losing my powers at a time when I needed them most. If you fail when crossing the abyss, two things can happen. First, you can bounce right back to the beginning and lose all your powers. Second, you can fall into the pit – then it's goodbye world.

'With the arrival of these new people, things started to go wrong. I found I couldn't do the tarot readings anymore. The crystal ball didn't work . . . .'

Jim later learned that the three new residents were all Christians. One is now a Church of England minister and another was the girl he eventually married, Veronica.

Ouija boards

New people entering into the occult are reassured that ouija is a genuine part of the occult, despite its being hijacked as a family board game by Waddingtons House of Games. The company later withdrew this from the high street stores and from its production schedule, following a large number of complaints from Christian individuals and groups. A company spokesman was not able to say whether or not the two were connected.

Ouija is made up of the French and German words for 'yes', and this would suggest that it was originally an 'answering machine' for the spirits of the board. The operators would ask questions and a wooden tripod on wheels would be guided to the correct answer. A refinement of this, a mounted pencil on castors, was invented in 1853 by a French spiritualist called Planchette. Today, the ouija is usually a board displaying the alphabet, the numerals up to 9, and other symbols. The participants place their fingers on the top of an upturned glass or pointer on castors. History has seen many types of spirit 'answering machines' including table rapping or tipping (each rap or tilt spelling out a letter or answer) and pendulum swinging over an alphabet. The ouija board has proved the most enduring.

It is thought that perhaps as many as twenty million have been sold across America and Europe in the last forty years to people anxious to contact dead relatives or to get answers to difficult problems in life.

There are four main theories of what causes movement on a ouija board:

1. Involuntary physical movements of one or more of the participants. It is difficult to control one's arms after prolonged suspension over an object. This has to be ruled out when the movement of the glass begins to make sense of letters, and even phrases.

2. Deliberate deception. It is not unknown for practical jokers – among both dabblers and serious occultists – to have fun at the expense of others. This can generally be ruled out when answers or messages include private details known only to one participant. On occasions, the personal information revealed has been highly embarrassing for one of the circle, according to reports of those counselled. Telepathy (mind reading) is another possible explanation when personal facts are unveiled, and this we shall cover more fully in Chapters 12 and 13.

3. The subconscious of one or more of the participants. This occurs when the deep desires, frustrations and fantasies of the hidden self effervesce to the surface. Even private and personal information can evade the conscious controls or natural brakes, and an individual's subconscious will transmit information that the conscious mind would otherwise never dream of releasing. Without the devil or demons being involved, the ouija board can act as stageprop to inspire the subconscious of the weak-minded and susceptible.

John Allan, an experienced Christian in the field of parapsychology and the deliverance ministry, spoke to me of his fears in this area. He said, 'It is possible to bypass the censor which normally filters the impulses deriving from our subconscious, and let out things which ought to be kept in. In fact I think there is overwhelming evidence to show that at least some of the time a ouija board can be a device (like a crystal ball or a pendulum) for releasing the forces of the subconscious in an irresponsible way, which can cause untold damage to the human personality.'

Surprisingly, those in the occult could be similarly quoted, as in a Tyne Tees television programme broadcast live on Halloween, 1987. A variety of witches faced us across the TV studio and encouraged us by supporting our warning to the public to avoid playing around with the ouija board. One witch said, 'It is a powerful tool in the occult and we would also warn anybody who does not know what they are doing to stay well clear of the ouija.'

A few days before the broadcast I had been counselling one man in his early twenties who would also have issued the same warning. He vowed to break his association with the board after being thrown back from it several feet across the room.

4. Ouija can attract an external and evil guiding intelligence. When dealing with those adversely affected by the occult and in need of deliverance, the ouija board is one constantly arising factor in their sad histories. In the last decade, the ouija board has been a feature in several serious crimes. I record three notable and recent ones.

The Glasgow High Court heard in January 1986 of the couple who were obsessed by the ouija board, tarot cards and the occult. The twenty-three-year-old woman said that her spirit guide, a Tibetan monk, told her, 'Your child has to die.' She tried to strangle her three-month-old daughter and then her lover arrived to finish the evil deed.

At Gloucester Crown Court in August 1986 a young mother was found guilty of killing her four-year-old son whom she believed to be the devil. The court was told that she dabbled in black magic and tried summoning messages from the spirit world by using a ouija board. This led her to believe that her younger son, Ryan, was Jesus reborn and that four-year-old Ben was Satan. She told the court that to save Ryan she had to kill Ben. She stabbed Ben to death with a pair of dress-making scissors and then tried to kill herself.

On a less tragic but equally terrifying note, a family fled from their Worcester home in February 1986 to stay with relatives until the council could find them another house. They allowed a council-appointed paranormal expert into their home to investigate a nine-month haunting. They had lived in fear after hearing many noises and seeing objects fly across rooms. The expert used a ouija board in an attempt to contact the spirit that was believed to be tormenting them. The board spelled out *FIRE*, confirming the family's fear that the spirit meant them harm. The family refused to be reassured by the expert's promises that poltergeists did not harm people.

The ultimate warning over ouija comes from a high-ranking chaos magician who knew I was writing this book. He wrote, 'Please point out that many occultists also condemn the ouija board in untrained hands, though not for your reasons.'

Personal effects

You will recall those frequent stories of psychics who are called in, often by the police, to locate missing bodies. They often require an article belonging to the missing person to aid them, or to act as a 'prop' for their psychic powers.

In fairness, some psychics believe that the personal effects are more than 'props'. They generally believe in a cosmic memory (known officially as psychometry). It is the occult theory that physical objects are imprinted with their own history, and that of their owners. Each object is said to possess, or be part of the Akasha, which to some is a universal 'ether' in which the world's events are said to be recorded. To others, it relates to the 'quintessence', the luminous and invisible fifth element that binds together the normal four elements of earth, air, fire and water.

Cosmic memory is perhaps the oldest fortune-telling method known to man. By handling an object, it is said that the sensitive person can not only identify its owner, but describe his character and even his whereabouts. The theory was first put forward by H R Buchanan in his *Manual of Psychometry* in 1889, when he argued that all objects contain the history of the world because they are connected to the Akashic Chronicles. These chronicles, he said, were a universal ether–library with records of every personal experience, thought and deed that had ever happened. His argument was based on personal opinion, feelings and intuition though it does have a loose connection to Carl Gustav Jung's theory of racial memory, which has fallen into disuse in modern times.

Many psychics pay lip service to the Akasha theory. They prefer to use personal articles of missing owners as 'props' to assist their gifts of telepathy and clairvoyance (see Chapter 12). Some use the articles as a focus to call up guiding spirits of the cosmic force.

Voodoo dolls

Ten years ago not many authors, Christian or otherwise, would have included voodoo in an English book on the occult. Today it is increasingly surfacing in our country. It is tied in with sympathetic magic which has been an enduring part of the British occult scene for many centuries. One of the key elements of voodoo and sympathetic magic involves the manufacture of a wax or clay image of a person the magician wishes to influence. This poppet, as it is called, is then damaged in an appropriate way, if the magician wishes a person harm. Alternatively, it is treated pleasantly and gently if the magician wishes to secure a person's co-operation. Its most popular usage is in rituals to obtain sexual favours.

Voodoo has been a contributing factor in many horrendous incidences in the United Kingdom in recent years. Here are some of the most recent criminal court cases.

In July, 1986 the Old Bailey witnessed the trial of a woman branded 'voodoo child killer' by the press. She was eventually given two life sentences for murdering her seven–year–old daughter and her four-year-old playmate. She strangled the two girls, hid their bodies and then played the distraught mother making impassioned pleas for the return of her 'abducted' children. At the trial, the mother's defence was that she was haunted by black magic and voodoo, and a voice had commanded her to 'Strangle! Strangle!'

A London male prostitute knitted a voodoo doll out of black wool before killing his flatmate, an Old Bailey judge was told in February 1987. The doll had pins piercing the location of the heart when the police found it lying on the victim's naked body. The accused, who pleaded guilty, said, 'I felt the devil and his horns on my head when I plunged the knife through his heart.'

London's Kingston Crown Court jailed an American and her lover for deception in December 1986. Waiting in the court were two officers with extradition warrants in case the couple were set free. They are wanted back in the States for the 'voodoo murders' of the girl's parents.

Interpol, at the time of writing, were looking for a Norfolk widow regarding their enquiries into the death of her husband. Police found his body buried in a back-garden cesspit, and the widow was last seen by her next-door neighbour doing a 'voodoo dance in the garden with blood smeared on the doorsteps'.

Conclusion

Sympathetic magic and voodoo, with their dolls, are two of many more systems which use 'props' for contacting and manipulating the forces of evil. There are a large number of other methods we could examine. For instance, there are more than sixty separate forms of divination.[5] The occult even stoops to necromancy, the claimed practice of calling back into temporary life a dead body for the purposes of extracting information out of its spirit. No matter which method we look at, the overall principle remains the same. The methods and their paraphernalia are all 'stageprops', aids to contacting the same force and channelling the mind in that direction.

11

Package Tours into Inner Space

Excursions into inner space are proving far more dangerous than man's ventures into outer space. Increasingly man is being urged to launch himself into the barely-explored regions of his innermost self in 'crafts' which are often unstable. The first modern pioneers began to probe inner space more than a century ago, but the data are still highly speculative, confusing, contradictory, and with a marked absence of hard facts. Despite these great dangers, hypnotists, Transcendental Meditation gurus, parapsychologists, occultists and spiritualists, among others, are now offering 'package tours' for all who wish to venture into the great interior. Often there are no tour guides and travellers are getting lost, or returning with spiritual, mental and sometimes physical distress.

The Bishop of Peterborough in his diocesan magazine warned of the dangers of playing with the occult and the unknown. He stated that he had met too many people who had become mentally disturbed by playing about with ideas and activities which have done them deep emotional damage.[1]

The Archbishop of Canterbury warned of the deliberate worship of evil through spiritualism and the occult. He also warned that it was neither obscure nor medieval.

'There is today,' he explained, 'a dangerous fascination with demonic devotion and ritual, and reports of their beguiling, destructive effects seem all too frequent.'[2]

The Evangelical Alliance, representing more than a million Christians of all denominations, was so concerned over the increasing problems created by the occult that it published *Doorways to Danger*. In it Christian psychiatrists, care workers, medical experts, ministers and those who had come out of the occult scene, spoke of the appalling wake of damage left by the occult.[3]

Since the mid–seventies, each Church of England diocese has had an individual or small group to cope with the victims of the occult. This is also true, although in a more limited way, for the free church denominations. These ministries, many of the exorcists tell me, are being used increasingly each year.

So far in this book, we have looked at some of the more dangerous types of 'vehicle' used for inner-space exploration such as satanism, witchcraft, New Age paganism and occult magic. Chaos magic is probably the most irresponsible way of launching people into the void of inner space. In this chapter, I attempt a kind of *Which?* report on the supposedly more respectable forms of interior travel. Often they are cloaked in the respectability of scientific terminology or social acceptability.

Transcendental Meditation (TM)

This is so respectable today that Christians of all denominations have embraced it. There is now a Christian TM Group based at Harbourne Hall, Birmingham, 'which seeks to promote . . . a clearer understanding of the value of TM for spiritual growth.'[4] A 1983 book entitled *TM: An Aid to Christian Growth* was reprinted in 1987. The contributors, Roman Catholic priests and TM teachers among them, sought to harmonise the teaching of the Maharishi Mahesh Yogi with their own views of Christianity.

They regretted TM's 'eastern mystical' connotations but pointed out that it was 'a very simple, natural technique which allows mental activity to settle down to a state of increased inner quietness, producing deep mental and physical rest'.[5] It was not an hypnotic trance, they stressed, and the mind remained fully alert during the two twenty-minute daily sessions. They denied that TM was addictive or produced 'spiritual trips', or that it was viewed as a way of saving themselves by their own efforts. It was stressed that, for the Christian, TM led to a greater awareness and devotion of many aspects of scriptural faith. The contributors suggested that Christianity needed TM because it was 'the most direct way to gain a deeper state of inner quietness'. In short, it was claimed that meditators' moral senses were enlivened and it helped them 'become better Christians'.[6]

The contributors' arguments became a little less convincing when they came to explain why mantras were used. To many in the occult, a mantra is a meaningless sound, the resonance of which has a soothing effect on the body. However, many of the innumerable mantras are, in fact, the names of fourth-class deities in Hinduism. A mantra is given to a trainee meditator when his teacher initiates him into TM during an eastern ritual. This ceremony, called *puja*, involves the recitation of a long list of seers and gods to show the 'pedigree' of a mantra. Christian TM practitioners insist that a fourth-class god in Hinduism is not an actual deity but part of mythical folk lore.[7] A later contributor in the above book recognises the weaknesses of this argument when he suggests that TM should be modified to suit various cultures.[8] Another contributor, however, says that 'Maharishi lays so much stress on the sound value of the mantra, and its vibratory effect, that without it, you just would not be practising TM.'[9]

'Please note,' requested a TM official, 'that a mantra is only the equivalent of prayer with a fixed wording.' The question arises: at whom then are the prayers aimed? From my understanding, more than a quarter of a million TM practitioners in England are in ignorance, currently invoking heathen deities twice a day, and the majority do not even know it!

There is little said about what is called the messianic role of TM in the book, apart from a token two pages. The Skelmersdale Transcendental Meditation project, mentioned in Chapter 9, is part of a structuring of TM teachers into National and World Governments of the Age of Enlightenment, complete with all sorts of ministries or responsibilities. Full-time workers are engaged to promote 'The Maharishi Effect' – the theory that a community or area will be changed for the better if one per cent of the population meditates. One of these promoters assured me that there were now more than thirty scientific surveys (carried out by TM) to 'prove', among other things, that accident and crime statistics dropped in areas where one per cent (or even the square root of one per cent) of the population were TM followers. However, he failed to point out that the same trends could equally be the result of a large variety of other factors. This eastern technique is being marketed as a way of salvation for society. Our Christian contributors choose to dismiss this by claiming that not many practitioners take this part of TM seriously. The TM public relations office, however, claimed that many were involved in the secondary form of TM.

The fact that TM has its direct roots in the Vedic Scriptures – the basis of Hinduism – is also brushed aside as irrelevant. The contributors follow the modern theory that Christians need to discover the areas in which the Holy Spirit has been at work in heathen faiths. Their belief is that TM should be recognised as the work of God's Spirit.[10] It seems a dangerous belief considering the numerous warnings in Scripture for Christians to avoid 'different gospels' and 'false prophets' and 'being unequally yoked with non-believers'

(Galatians 1:8; Acts 13:6; 2 Corinthians 6:14). It is hardly likely that the Holy Spirit would inspire those directions in his word, and then promptly break them with his deeds. To be sure, God's Spirit is at work in the East and everywhere, but that is different from saying that he contributes to beliefs which deny the truth that he has inspired.

Perhaps the greatest difficulty concerning TM is the TM-Sidhi Programme. Siddhis[11] are the powers which can be added on to basic TM such as levitation, extra-sensory perception, telepathy, telekinesis, spiritual healing and control of mind over body. The most well-known and televised of the TM powers is the 'flying' siddhi – the practice of 'leapfrogging' along with legs folded in the traditional Buddha posture. One Christian contributor writes of this, 'It produces a rapid expansion of one's ability to act from a deeper level of consciousness. It can also be extremely enjoyable to perform, incidentally.'[12] Apart from the 'flying' siddhi, the remainder are psychic gifts and we shall be looking at this area in the next two chapters. We have already noted in an earlier chapter that meditation, along with yoga, is recognised by modern occultists as one of the four main paths of magic.

Before leaving TM, Christians need to accept part of the blame for its popularity. Man is a spiritual animal and will seek spiritual satisfaction elsewhere if Christianity does not provide it. Transcendental Meditation would have remained in the East if Western Christianity had not forgotten the mysticism of meditation. Men and women need a peaceful time to be still and know the presence of God. We need biblical ways of practising the presence of God and to listen to him in the power of his Spirit. Somehow in this mad modern world we have lost this and, if nothing else, TM should inspire us to rediscover a biblical form of Christian meditation.

Yoga

This is a Sanskrit term meaning 'union' and is part of the Hindu philosophy of self-discipline which teaches self-control, with the aim of becoming one with the impersonal god force. It is developed from an eastern world view, and each of the postures adopted is still used in the East to invoke various deities. A Christian authority on eastern religions, Patrick Sookhdeo said, 'I have seen that whenever a person uses yoga, he makes a shift from a monotheistic view of God, to a pantheistic view (God identified with nature), and finally to a monistic view (God as an impersonal *IT*, without form, personality and essence). You have your basic yoga techniques – the Lotus posture. Your fingers shape a circle. What does that imply? The wheel, the unbrokenness of life; life in an unending cycle. Can Christians believe that?'[13]

The occult views yoga as a system of mind-control, and the postures adopted are to facilitate certain types of breathing to help the practitioner get in union with the force. For them, yoga is as powerful as any other path of magic, though it takes longer to achieve magical results.[14] This path of magic is recommended to the quiet, pacifistic person who dislikes the dramatic and likes to allow the world to take its own time.

The average person who practises keep-fit or lessen-stress yoga (*hatha yoga*) will wonder what all the fuss is about. He or she will probably have never heard of magic or the pagan philosophies undergirding yoga exercises. Most will have started yoga after watching it on television or because a friend invited them to join a local group. The members spend their evenings twisting and stretching on their mats. Occasionally the teacher goes into some 'funny explanations', but apart from that they do yoga for health of body and mind.

However, what many yoga fans will have heard about is the 'life-force', especially if they followed Richard Hittleman's *Yoga for Health* series on television.

'I have explained both in previous chapters and during our programmes,' he writes in his best-selling book which accompanies the series, 'that from the yoga viewpoint, all life is sustained by a force which the Yogis have named *prana*. We can translate this Sanskrit word *prana* (literally 'breath') into English by using the term life-force .... One of the most important yoga techniques consists of directing the life-force .... All living things must continually receive life-force to sustain themselves .... If you comply with its needs, the Yogi believes you will succeed in your yoga practice and that you will grow mentally, emotionally and spiritually .... The yoga formula is as follows: the more life-force, the more awareness of life and all its implications; the less life-force, the less sense of life and the realisation of its meaning and purpose.'[15]

A good, old-fashioned keep-fit session seems much healthier than Hindu-inspired life-force exercises which were originally designed as an act of worship to thousands of eastern gods. Yoga has too many unfortunate non-Christian connotations, not least of which is the unhelpful eastern view of right and wrong. Right is equated with enlightenment and knowledge of the life-force. Sin is regarded as ignorance of it. Again, the average yoga keep-fit enthusiast will not meet this concept at the beginning. But he will before long. It is built into a world view which, given time, rarely fails to bubble up.

Hypnotism

My first doubts about hypnotism surfaced twenty years ago in a Manchester nightclub. At the time I was in public relations with the old National Coal Board, and we had hired the services of a club hypnotist to entertain some of our clients and agents. I entered into the spirit of the occasion by volunteering as one of about twenty stage guinea pigs, but within minutes I had been weeded out and sent back to my seat. Six remained to 'perform' for a delighted audience. One believed himself to be Mario Lanza, and, at the mention of a 'key' word, would assault a well-known aria in a way that would have peeled the paint off any bathroom wall. A second 'entranced' victim kept leaping for cover every time the hypnotist mentioned another special word. The victim had been told, while in trance, that the word would remind him that he had come out without his trousers! The poor man was exhausted by the end of the performance and his cardigan looked like a sack! It had been constantly pulled down to cover his imagined embarrassment. The laughter faded away, leaving me with a sense of unease. It was only years later, after becoming a Christian, that I was able to clothe that feeling with words.

It must be stressed that there are important differences between stage hypnotism and the techniques used in alternative medicine. But the entertaining variety does help to illustrate a basic problem common to all hypnotism.

The 'victim' of the stage hypnotist was brought out of his trance before he was incited to perform outrageous actions which he would never have contemplated in normal circumstances. On one level, the victim's mind was operating normally. He was able to keep control of himself until the hypnotist mentioned a code-word. This then suggested an altered reality in the victim's mind. He believed his circumstances had changed. The singer, for instance, believed himself to be a great tenor performing before an adoring audience at La Scala.

This raises the evergreen question of whether or not a person's will can be affected by hypnosis? The popular belief is that it cannot. I have been reassured on countless occasions that a hypnotist cannot make me do anything against my will. I remain unconvinced. I would agree that a hypnotist could not, for example, make me attack an innocent person. This would be against my nature. However, I do strongly suspect that he could change my perspective of reality so as to make it extremely difficult not to attack the person. Under hypnosis, he could suggest, for instance, that this person was going to kill my wife and children and that, as a good Christian, I could not possibly allow that to happen. In this way, the hypnotist is not making me attack against my will, he is conjuring up a set of circumstances in which to attack seems the lesser of two evil courses.

In hypnosis, I retain my ability to choose which actions I wish to execute. What I lose is my full ability to monitor and assess correctly a given situation. Martin and Deidre Bobgan in their booklet *Hypnosis and the Christian* state,

> The monitoring function helps us in making decisions by comparing past situations to the current situation. Such recall of information and application to the present situation may change our decision on how to act . . . . Since reality becomes distorted during a trance, the subject cannot properly evaluate which actions make sense and which ones do not.[16]

Perhaps the greatest problem with hypnotism concerns man's ignorance. Scientists are still unable to tell us what it is or even how it works. We are therefore exploring inner space in a vehicle which is alien and with only limited knowledge of its controls. Much medical opinion also assures us that hypnosis is not essential. Equally satisfactory results can be obtained using more orthodox treatments.

There is also concern with the use of deception to induce hypnosis. Hynotists are taught 'double bind' talk to gain the confidence of patients. In layman's language, this means that every reaction of the patient is regarded as the right reaction. Every twitch, blink, yawn and movement is used to tell the patient that he is responding correctly. If a hypnotist is willing to be so deceptive while hypnotising a patient, can he be trusted when the patient is in a trance?

Let us imagine that you have found a hypnotist who is honest. You trust him not to lead you astray either en route to the trance or while in it. Can a Christian in this case be hypnotised? This becomes a possibility. However, you then have another problem called the placebo effect. You believe in the hypnotist and believe that he can help you. Your faith then may become the dominant factor in any healing that might take place. Faith plays an enormous part in healing. Doctors can convince trusting patients that they will get better even while giving them a course of pills which consist of little more than sugar and water. It is well-known in orthopaedic hospitals that mentally sub-normal people with broken bones recover fifteen to twenty per cent faster than normal patients. Their trust can so easily be won by the surgeons and nurses, and it is the absence of anxiety and worry which enable bones to knit together faster.

Not only does the trusting Christian need to worry about the placebo effect, he also needs to be aware that he will want to please his therapist, having placed so much faith in him. If the hypnotist does not turn out to be as trustworthy as expected, this can be extremely dangerous.

Regression hypnotism provides the Christian with his greatest worry. Therapists will take a patient back to difficult areas of the past, if they believe that the patient's problems stem from this. Less reputable hypnotists may then try to change the facts. The girl who was beaten up, for instance, may be urged to reconstruct the incident in a way that is less traumatic than it originally was. She may even be asked to visualise the whole incident in a different way. She then returns to full consciousness with her past subtly changed. Can a distortion of past events really produce a healthy outlook on life? It seems extremely doubtful. The patient ends up not knowing how to differentiate between what are her own thoughts, and those which have been implanted. The therapist becomes a 'con' man, and the patient the dupe! That seems a recipe for a mental breakdown.

Regression therapy can also involve taking a patient back into the womb. Returning to the original metaphor of this chapter, the patient is taken into dangerous and unexplored territories of inner space. They are being used as the 'guinea pigs' of inner space exploration!

The whole of this area is a maelstrom of medical 'meteorites', all coming from different directions. Martin and Deidre Bobgan believe that a baby or foetus has no capacity to record and store information.

'The myelin sheathing,' they write, 'is too underdeveloped in the prenatal, natal and early postnatal brain to store such memories.'[17] This, of course, begs the question: if the source of information concerning life in the womb and at birth cannot possibly be of the patient, then who – or what – else could be the origin?

The opponents who refute the Bobgans' claim include Dr Thomas Verny[18] and Christian clinical theologian Frank Lake.[19] These and others maintain that a human being can be affected by events, emotions and environment from conception onwards. Frank Lake insists that counselling must take account of these pre-birth traumas. Those on this side of the argument would refute any suggestion that prenatal knowledge comes from any other source than the patient himself.

Whichever side is right, do hypnotists have the right to take patients into potentially dangerous, unknown areas of inner space? Personally, I am rather too fond of my sanity to risk it in this way.

The real problems start when the hypnotist regresses a patient back to 'previous lives' which have supposedly been lived on earth or on another planet. In this realm, there is no controversy between Christians, only the certainty of doubtful origins. This is especially true when the information given by the patient turns out to be astonishingly accurate, as on numerous occasions. The occultist would label the source as 'psychic'. The Christian would be more inclined to call it 'satanic'. This is dealt with more fully in the next chapter.

I have written of hypnotism with fear and trepidation. I am conscious of many in history who have opposed advances in medicine, and of the pioneers who have struggled on against difficult odds. However, if a church member asks whether or not it is right for a Christian to be hypnotised, I have to give a negative answer. I would then go on to provide a more positive option. We are now blessed with a growing number of Christian counselling and pastoral care services in England, such as Ellel Grange, near Lancaster. This residential healing centre has proved a great blessing to many of my friends. They, along with a growing number of church ministries, are able to minister in the power of the Holy Spirit with notable success. The ministry of Christian healing and deliverance introduces the missing part to the incomplete picture of modern and alternative medicine. It reintroduces God, who created life, and who has no problem repairing it when it goes wrong.

Freemasonry

Does this surprise you? What, you may ask, have the masons to do with 'package tours into inner space', or paganism or the occult for that matter?

The answer can be stated quickly: masons were the original modern pioneers of the occult voyages into 'inner space', according to several sources. First, we will deal with the original occult links of freemasonry. Secondly, we will look at the pagan links via the mason's name for God. Finally, we will conclude with a brief review of freemasonry today.

The occult connection

To be fair to the United Grand Lodge of England, let me first start with a denial. Grand Lodge Librarian and Curator John Hamill made it his first priority to assure me that 'freemasonry contains neither pagan nor occult practices'. He also dismissed the allegation – popular with some Christian mason-watchers – that freemasonry was founded in an 'antiquity that goes back into pagan religions well before the birth of Christ'. He would also refute the suggestion that the ancestors of the Craft were Druids or ancient Egyptians. Grand Lodge are appalled by the often-used argument that modern freemasonry was founded by middle-class gentlemen who wanted a secret society to study alchemy and the occult.

'What is true,' writes mason investigator Stephen Knight, 'is that the philosophic, religious and ritualistic concoction that makes up the speculative element in freemasonry is drawn from many sources – some of them, like the Isis-Osiris myth, dating back to the dawn of history. Rosicrucianism, Gnosticism, the Kabbala, Hinduism, Theosophy and traditional notions of the occult all play a part.'[20]

Mr Hamill, the masons' own leading historian, would be the first to acknowledge that there is no certainty concerning the origins of the Craft. The founding brothers never entrusted anything to paper, fearing that rituals and their interpretation of them might fall into the wrong hands.

One long-standing allegation of satanic elements in masonry, however, still awaits a satisfactory answer. Lady Queensborough claimed that the masonic god was revealed in the highest degrees as Lucifer. She claimed to be quoting from the highest rituals when she wrote,

The Masonic Religion should be by all of us initiates of the high degrees maintained in the purity of the Luciferian doctrine.[21]

Grand Lodge, in its evidence to a 1987 Church of England Working Party set up to investigate whether or not Christianity and freemasonry were compatible, claimed that this was wrong.

'This is a typical example of the Judeo-Masonic-Communist-Occult world domination plot school of conspiracy,' they claimed, adding that the Lady's scholarship was 'based on unreliable and hostile secondary sources'. The Lodge also said that her reasoning was 'inaccurate and biased', and went on to imply that she was a Fascist who could not be trusted.[22]

They did not, however, deny the above quote, allegedly taken from the 30th, 31st and 32nd degrees. Surely, the most effective denial of this satanic allegation would have been to allow the rituals of the higher degrees to be published in full.

What is known is that the founder-members of this century's most influential occult order, The Golden Dawn,[23] were all high-ranking masons. These included Dr William Woodman, McGregor Mathers, Wynn Westcott in 1877 and, later, Aleister Crowley.[24]

Before continuing, it must be noted that though all free-masonry flows from similar origins, they are not all under the jurisdiction of the United Grand Lodge of England. The above named were members of the Ancient and Accepted Rite of Freemasonry (a Scottish degree which originated from the continent).

R G Torrens in his book on the inner teachings of the Golden Dawn implies that all masonry once had the dark occult secrets, but had 'become . . . an empty form'. The real secret of masonry had been lost, he wrote, and could now only be found in other organisations faithful to the Ancient Mysteries. Torrens also points out that many of the early masonic lodges were 'orientated to the setting or rising sun' and 'others were aligned to receive the light from certain stars'. This was done to 'focus light from one of the heavenly bodies, direct and unpolluted, into the Holy of Holies over the heads of the assembled congregation'. He adds that 'anyone who has knowledge of masonic working in the higher degrees, will mark a part of one ceremony which maintains a record of this in its ritual.'[25]

Mason Grand Masters were also responsible for the founding and structure of one of Europe's largest occult societies, the Ordo Templi Orientis (OTO) in 1902.[26] Around the turn of the century, there was much disenchantment with freemasonry because it was negating its original secrets of the occult and becoming more a social club and friendly society. In 1904, the OTO announced the nature of its teachings in the society's organ *Oriflamme*.

'Our Order possesses the KEY,' claimed the article, 'which opens up all Masonic and Hermetic secrets, namely, the teaching of sexual magic, and this teaching explains, without exception, all the secrets of Nature, all the symbolism of FREEMASONRY and all systems of religion' [their capital letters].[27]

I have in my possession the OTO's own list of 'Administrative and governmental offices and official bodies as of 5/15/87' showing it to be a worldwide network of undercover occultism. I also have its organisation flow up to 1969 when many OTO lodge members were arrested and sentenced for child abuse in California. By this time the organisational history had become vague and shrouded in mystery. The British headquarters is given only as The OTO Oasis, BM Box 3338, London, WC1N 3XX.

Maury Terry, an award-winning journalist, published in 1987 *The Ultimate Evil*, his investigation into the 'deadly satanic cults' which involved the OTO.[28] His interest began after David Berkowitz was arrested for the Son of Sam murders, one of the most notorious murder cases in US criminal history. It was linked with the Manson murders in 1969 and several other horrific crimes. Far below the surface, Terry found 'an infinitely more frightening spectre – that of a network of Satan-worshipping cults that criss-crossed the United States.'

The occult position, helped by the OTO, has become so acute in the States that police are now thankful to attend seminars on satanism. In 1987, 120 members of the New York City Police Department attended one such day-long course conducted by the Interfaith Coalition for Concern

About Cults. Here in England, few police officers will even acknowledge that satanism is a reality. One officer explained to me that it would not help their credibility nor their promotion prospects if they were too closely identified with investigations into the occult. A Northern force faced with several desecrated graveyards and missing bodies in 1986 found it easier to describe it as the work of vandals. There was a similar reaction after several bodies went missing from Britain's biggest cemetery in Surrey in April 1988, even after a man had been arrested and charged for decapitating a disinterred corpse.

The OTO, founded by freemasons, has much to answer for in the last eighty years.

The pagan connection

In the past, freemasons have labelled and slandered the Christian God by reducing him to a miniature deity. The mason god has been a Hebrew-Syriac-Egyptian mixture by the name of JAH–BUL–ON.

This is the composite word on the triangle which is the central focus of every Royal Arch chapter.[29] The letters have, until recently, invariably been accepted as the name of God in three languages. Even as late as 1984, the Revd Francis Heydon, the then Third Grand Principal of Grand Lodge, gave this interpretation.[30] It has led critics to accuse, with good reason, the Craft of mixing the Biblical God JAH (YHWH or Jehovah) with the Syriac god BUL (or Baal) and the Egyptian god ON (or Osiris).

In recent years, several major Christian denominations have criticised freemasonry for this pagan trinity, and other matters.[31] It has provoked freemasonry to examine itself and nurtured a desire for a new image.

'Tradition dies hard and it may well be that many zealous companions will go on quoting Syriac and Egyptian and perpetuating this extraordinary jumble of explanations,' wrote Canon Richard Tydeman, Grand Superintendent over the Suffolk province of Freemasonry, in 1985. 'I will not say that they are wrong but I will say that I think they are definitely unwise in the present climate of opinion . . . . It is certainly not expedient to lay ourselves open to charges of idolatry or syncretism at a time when churches are seriously examining our beliefs and doctrines.'[32]

Canon Tydeman went on to offer an alternative interpretation of JAH–BUL–ON. He said that they should be taken all from the Hebrew language. He then explained that ' . . . what we are pronouncing are not the three names of God (or worse still the names of three gods, as some would suggest) but we are pronouncing three aspects or qualities of the Deity which are well-known and used, in Christianity and other religions, namely His Eternal Existence, His Transcendence and His Omnipotence.'

Christian mason-watcher John Lawrence has his doubts:

'The fact that it [JAH–BUL–ON] stands at the pinnacle of Craft Freemasonry makes it well nigh impossible to change. It is an idol, a false, man-made attempt at redefining God, and its position at the very heart of the Craft, as the innermost secret, simply serves to show how freemasonry stands on a spurious foundation.'[33]

Present-day freemasonry

Freemasonry in England has negotiated a remarkable U-turn in the last three years due to the criticisms of church, state, its own embarrassed members, the police, the Press and the general public. Out has gone the traditional 'no comment' to be replaced by an almost 'open door' policy. Commander Michael Higham, Grand Secretary, believes that freemasonry has become a 'convenient whipping post' mainly because it has refused to answer its critics.[34] Following widespread unfavourable publicity, Grand Lodge decided to redefine its rules on public relations in 1984.[35]

The vast majority of masons today are genuinely puzzled at the criticisms of the last decade. Those who live around me in Grand Lodge's two largest provinces, East and West Lancashire (where 15% of the country's 320,000 masons live), would be horrified to read of their Craft's occult and pagan links. They consider themselves to be pillars of society with long-standing royal patronage and a fine reputation for giving away millions of pounds in charity. They point out that fellow brothers include the directors of all big companies, many of the doctors, accountants and solicitors, and a large percentage of church leaders (lay and clergy). One provincial officer asked me, 'How much more respectable can you be?'

Conclusion

There is an inherent incompatibility between freemasonry and Christianity. The two cannot go together because of fundamental differences. This is not only a personal view but also that of many Christian denominations.[36] Freemasonry has been criticised, with good reasons, for its false god, its inaccurate gospel,[37] its secrecy and, consequently, its easy abuse, its confusion of Scripture with its own ancient myths and fables,[38] and its susceptibility to being misused for members' selfish ends.

The origins of freemasonry, even though those in the occult may dismiss the Craft as an 'empty form', are most certainly not of God. We have argued from Scripture in this book that there is only one alternative source – Satan. For the following reasons, I believe that it is still under its original controller:

1. I have had to minister to several who have felt oppressed by their connection with freemasonry. One woman, a vicar's wife, spoke of her involvement with, and influence of her high-ranking masonic father. Following her conversion to Christianity, she underwent a ministry of deliverance after experiencing oppression.

'I didn't understand why I needed it,' she told me, 'but when the minister prayed over me, it was just like a weight being lifted right off.'

Several former masons, or close relatives of those still in the Brotherhood, have spoken to me in similar ways. Some mentioned 'a sense of bondage' or 'a sense of evil'. The church of England Working Party on Freemasonry also received, and published, evidence of this nature. An ex-mason, who gave his evidence to the working party, wrote of 'a beautiful sense of lightness and freedom I experienced when that oppression was lifted.'[39]

2. Whenever a church leadership is dominated by free-masons, I find a dead tradition and lifeless ritual. More often than not it is lively on the social side, but spiritually dead. It has no vision and no sense of God's leadership.

This, of course, could be a coincidence. But I think not. Nor do the dozens of other Bible-believing Christians with whom I have discussed the matter. All from personal experience agree that freemasonry brings the end of spiritual life in a church.

3. Freemasonry claims the first loyalty of men. Perhaps Christianity has been to blame for not providing manly worship and interests and fellowship. Leading evangelist Jim Smith certainly thinks so, causing him to write three books on how the church can reach out and hold men.[40] Having taken the plank out of our eye, we can see clearly how the Craft has stepped into the vacuum. Around my area, 50,000 men follow freemasonry and each has sworn to give his utmost allegiance to the Craft.

4. There can be no fellowship with darkness. The apostle Paul's warning to the Corinthians applies equally to our society:

What fellowship can light have with darkness? What harmony is there between Christ and Belial? What does a believer have in common with an unbeliever? What agreement is there between the temple of God and idols? . . . Therefore come out from them and be separate, says the Lord' (2 Cor 6:15–17).

12

Psychic Gifts

It was business as usual at the beginning of August 1987 for world-famous medium Doris Stokes – two months after her death! There was one obvious difference: she was coming through from the Other Side.

This was the claim of her friend and associate Lee Lacey who said that he had received messages of love from Doris during her memorial service at the Friends' Meeting House, Euston Road, London. She had revealed that she was surrounded by the spirits of her four dead children, her parents, and a host of spirit youngsters through whom she operated when she was on This Side. Asked why it had taken so long for Doris to get back in touch with this world, Mr Lacey explained that it was probably the exhaustion caused by her illness, the brain operation and unsuccessful medical treatment.

What's what in the psychic world?

Psychic gifts and phenomena are now all the rage in both the New Age and the occult. What are we to make of them? Before looking more closely at our departed medium Doris and other psychics and their phenomena, let us remind ourselves of the main areas.

Mediumship

The alleged ability, in or out of trance, to contact the spirit-world, usually during a seance. Some claim to extrude ectoplasm, the substance out of which spirits are said to be made. One medium even claimed to have made a plaster cast of a pair of ectoplasmic hands before they dissolved. There is no record of any laboratory tests on the substance though it has often been photographed. It is seen as a white, gooey substance, said to smell vaguely of ozone,[1] and is seen extruding from a medium's mouth or other natural orifice. It is said to be invisible in its natural state but will form into semi-matter under certain conditions, rather like invisible moist air condensing into a filmy liquid on windows.

Mediumship is famous for its frauds. They are often much more in contact with the spirit of materialism and money!

Spiritualism

More than seventy million follow this worldwide religion. The services can be similar to those of orthodox Christianity, except they are led by mediums, and the sermon is often replaced by a seance. Some treat Jesus as the greatest medium who ever lived while others accept him as 'the psychic Son of God'. Spiritualism began in a wooden hut in America on 31st March 1848, when the three Fox sisters – Kate, Margaret and Leah – claimed to receive messages from a murdered pedlar. Within a few months there were several dozen mediums offering their services. Margaret confessed shortly before her death that the whole thing had been a hoax. Was she trying to clear her conscience, or was it Margaret's final act of revenge on Leah who had grabbed all the glory?

Spiritism

Generally, the same as above minus the religious bits. It was the French version of Spiritualism with a strong emphasis on reincarnation.

Clairvoyants

Those who claim to see the past or future or to have clear sight or understanding of present events without the use of normal senses. The most numerous would more accurately be described as clairsentients; sensing things through their 'third eye' or 'sixth sense'. Others are clairaudients (hearing voices).

Precognition

The knowledge or vision of something which will occur in the future. People who foresee airplane disasters before they happen are said to have this gift.

Astral travel

You might call it dreaming in a vivid, realistic way, though the occultist would like to go further, and claim that it is the 'desire body' going on an independent solo excursion from the physical. A person with no connection with the occult can occasionally experience this when cat-napping during the day. The dream can seem so real that he believes himself to be wide awake. On suddenly realising he is dreaming, he may try to wake up only to find that his body seems paralysed. It then demands a mental fight to regain physical control. This is a normal vivid dream state and is a natural activity of the brain. Occultists and some clairvoyants claim that this is the astral body. It is said to be a luminous and dynamic nature capable of independent existence apart from its physical counterpart. The astral body is said to be attached to the physical by an invisible silver cord, although it is not clear how something can be invisible yet silver.

Out-of-the body experiences (OBEs)

Similar to astral travel but with differences. Many claim to have had these near death; floating near the ceiling while looking down at their dying (or clinically dead) physical frames. As with astral travel, some talk of being linked to their physical bodies by a filmy cord. Nearly all OBE patients tell of travelling along a dark tunnel towards a distant light. They emerge into a beautifully peaceful park or garden, usually meeting a benevolent old man, and then are sent back through the tunnel to return to the physical world. The resuscitated patients often speak of a great sense of disappointment and loss on waking. Medical theorists suggest that these experiences are actually hallucinations caused by the brain's mood-controlling limbic system being starved of oxygen. The practitioners of medicine on the other hand are not so certain. They have had to explain why patients can sometimes provide vivid descriptions of their own resuscitation, explaining how it was done, who was involved and even what was said.

Telepathy

Similar in some ways to clairvoyance, but it mainly involves communicating with somebody else without using normal senses. Clairvoyants and mediums are often rechristened mind-readers, especially by those who do not believe in a spirit-world. A common criticism is that their 'telepathy' is nothing more than mumbo-jumbo covering the clever 'detective' work of extracting clues and information from their naive victims. However, not all telepathy can be discounted in this way.

Trance-channelling

Sharon Gless, of television's *Cagney and Lacey* fame, collected her 1987 Emmy for the best actress category and gave much of the credit to Lazaris, her spirit guide. She explained that Lazaris came through to her via a medium who went into a trance, and had been helping her for the previous eight years. Shirley MacLaine, according to her autobiography, similarly relies on contacting disembodied entities through various mediums.[2]

Automatic writing

Receiving and writing messages from the spirit world (or the subconscious, depending on which occultist one is talking to). Often an entranced medium acts as a 'dictation machine' under direct control. Some act in a conscious state, more like shorthand-typists being guided by their spiritual bosses. Some see the ouija board as a 'machine' to facilitate this process. Much occult literature is said to have been written automatically. Brian Inglis, *The Times* reporter and television presenter, suggests in a recent book that some of our famous authors may not have actually written their bestsellers. Someone (or something) else may have been responsible. Graham Greene, for example, said that he wrote *The Confidential Agent* in record time under the influence of benzedrine. He said that it was like taking dictation, 'as if I was ghosting for another man'. Charles Dickens apparently claimed to hear every word he wrote. Henry Miller spoke of the time unseen powers dictated the *Tropic of Cancer* to him. Perhaps all this is no more than plain old-fashioned inspiration. Or is it always so plain?

Divination

This word embraces multifarious ways of looking into the future, consciously or unconsciously, generally enlisting the help of spirit beings.

Possession

This is a technical occult word used to describe the state of a person who has a demon in residence. The will of the person is under the demon's control, and this may also be true for the voice. Some claim that demons can even change the physical appearance of a host body. Exorcism is not limited to Christianity. Occultists also claim to cast out demons affecting or possessing one of their number, and even friends outside their magic circles. Most occultists would not agree with the Christian definition of a demon. To them, it is a product of the subconscious.

Ghosts and ghouls

The modern meaning of the first word usually relates to apparitions or spectres of dead people. Ghouls are more accurately evil spirits, believed to haunt graveyards and similar places, and to 'feed' on human remains. The word is Arabian and means 'to seize'.

A fish and chip shop owner called me in to deal with the lower half of a long-skirted ancestor which often glided through her kitchen. After several months, she felt it was time to lay the troublesome lady (and her own nerves) to rest. At the end of a short service of prayer, she wanted to know why half a lady should want to materialise in her kitchen. At that time, I trotted out the stock classical answer explaining that all events, especially those charged with high emotion, were permanently imprinted on the 'ether' or atmosphere of a place. It was similar to the tape recording process, and the 'machine' was always being replayed. Those who were psychically sensitive would occasionally be able to tune in to the 'replay'. Is it really an 'echo' from the past? Or could there be another explanation? We look at other possible answers in the next chapter.

Poltergeists

Seven or eight times out of ten, this is the phenomenon which greets those in the deliverance ministry when they are called on for help. The main features marking the presence of a poltergeist are moving objects, electrical high-jinks, or mysterious noises.

Local Christians took over our cinema to show the film *Jesus of Nazareth* and on the eve of the opening, the resident poltergeist threw a fit behind the closed doors of the projection room. The staff had heard it before on numerous occasions but nothing as severe or as noisy as on this particular night. When the caretaker eventually ventured into the room the following day, all was as usual.

Ask an occultist for an explanation and a variety will be offered. Some will speak of *elementars*, spiritual beings which invade the physical world from their normal residence in the astral plane. They might describe them as the unsettled 'shells' of the dead. Others will call them *Diakka*, unclean and amoral spirits, who take great delight in terrorising those who dabble in the spiritual phenomena without sufficient knowledge.

Ask a modern psychic and he will suggest that a poltergeist is no more than the manifesting energy of a disturbed human being. This theory became popular when it was observed that, in many cases, flying objects, noises and mischief all appeared to centre around an 'owner'. This was usually a person undergoing great emotional strain, such as a girl experiencing a particularly traumatic puberty.

Though many poltergeist influences can be explained in this way, what of those which happen in empty, uninhabited properties?

Psyche

To the Christian, this is the Greek word for soul, the essence of man. The occultist, thanks to Carl Gustav Jung as reinterpreted by Madam Blavatky and Theosophy, believe it is the animal and earthly nature of man. This nature is a dim refection of the great 'I' or Ego in the sky. There is a universal indestructible 'I' (called *Manas*) and each individual man is said to be merely a ray projected down from it.

Psychic (psi *for short*)

A psychic is one who senses by invisible means. He or she may be clairvoyant, a medium, or have a gift of telepathy. In fact, the psychic will be sensitive to most things in the above 'dictionary'.

Fact or fiction?

Doris Stokes claimed the attention of millions through her books, public hall seances and appearances on the television. She was a confidante to the stars including Coronation Street's Pat Pheonix, actor James Dean, and Elvis Presley. There were one hundred and fifty mourners at Doris's memorial service when Lee Lacey claimed to receive the messages from her. Is this another case of fraud? Was Mr Lacey making a take-over bid for Doris Stokes's empire? Or did Doris really come through? Are these gifts real?

From some of the illustrations we have already noted in our first chapter concerning Jeanne Dixon, there is circumstantial evidence to support these gifts. Mrs Dixon must either be 'in the know' from some source, or be incredibly good at guessing. It would, however, be much more convincing if we had proof positive: some sort of impartial and well-monitored test.

This was a line of thought pursued by scientist Peter Fairley, of the London *Evening Standard*, following the Aberfan disaster and the premonitions which preceded it. He began the Standard's Premonitions Bureau to record and date any claims of prophecies, and which would act only as an independent and impartial witness. The premonitions began to pour in about Grand National winners, storm warnings, earthquakes and other disasters. Not all were correct. But quite a few proved remarkably accurate. The bureau began to notice that some of their regular contributors were achieving higher-than-average success rates, and decided to investigate.

'The problem with all these stars,' said Peter Fairley, 'was that the moment they started to know that we were interested in what they could do, and we started to investigate how they did things, it just went. It has come through to me as a firm conclusion that, if there is such a thing as premonition, it is something which is instantaneous – a flash of intuition .... If you ask anyone to apply conscious thought to it, it just goes. The other conclusion is that, when it happens to you, it is an overpowering sensation. You *know* that it [the predicted event] is going to happen.'[4]

If the London Bureau can only provide circumstantial evidence, let us head north of the border to Edinburgh University and the chair of Britain's first Professor of Para-psychology. A quiet, bespectacled and sceptical American, Robert Morris, has spent the last few terms testing 'respondents' (the academics prefer this term to psychic, witch-doctor, shaman or whoever else they are analysing). Again, we come across tantalising circumstantial evidence, with the aid of standardised tests. All 'respondents' wear ear pads and ping-pong-ball goggles to ensure that their normal senses cannot operate. As a double precaution, they are locked in an electrically-shielded room. They are invited to sense sounds played in another room, or try to match patterned cards drawn elsewhere. Some 'respondents' have impressive scores, but these have never been sufficient to turn any academic hypothesis into theory, let alone fact.

The British Parapsychological Association received some bad news during their 1987 convention at the same university. Dr Susan Blackmore, of Bristol University, presented a controversial paper on the history of research into paranormal phenomena since 1880 and concluded, 'Psychical research has failed.' There was, she admitted, some evidence, but it had not resolved the controversy over the existence of the paranormal.

'We have no viable theory to account for the supposed phenomena and no technology at all,' Dr Blackmore stressed. 'We cannot produce or control them. We are still asking more or less the same questions we were a hundred years ago. And we still have no answers .... We have landed in a blind alley.'[5]

The doctor, like many scientists, returned to the only workable theory she knew: man was a brain in a body. Life ceased with the death of that body.

Many readers of our most respected newspaper *The Times* could not have disagreed more. Despite severe criticism, the newspaper conducted a poll in 1980 into the paranormal beliefs and experiences of its readers. The poll had inbuilt defects because the sample who replied were 'self-selecting'.[6]

Sixty-four per cent said they certainly believed psychic experiences existed and a further seventeen per cent thought them probable. Only two per cent thought they did not exist. Those who believed were asked to give their verdict on major psychic phenomena. The percentages are of those who believed they existed:

Extra-sensory perception	–	83%
Telepathy	–	83%
Contact with the dead	–	38%
Apparitions of the living	–	33%
Out-of-the-body experiences	–	54%
Reincarnation	–	29%
Haunting	–	53%
Poltergeists	–	52%
Dowsing[7]	–	70%
Precognition (premonitions)	–	73%

A similar poll was carried out among academics in the United States at about the same time. Half of them (about a thousand) thought that extra-sensory perception was a likely possibility and sixteen per cent believed that it was 'established fact'. As stated elsewhere in this book, a national opinion poll conducted by Southampton University and published on its 'Is Anyone There?' programme on Halloween 1987, showed that nine out of ten people in Britain believed in the reality of at least one psychic phenomenon.

Where do we go from here?

I have to confess at this point that my own sensitivity to psychic phenomena is scarcely higher than that of a slab of concrete. To be sure, I have had to deal with various phenomena and minister to those who have experienced them, and there have certainly been some chilling moments, but in general a ghost would have to flay me alive with its chains before I raised an eyebrow at the possibility of its presence. I have, however, experienced enough, and spoken to sufficient numbers of experienced psychics, to come to the private conclusion that the psychic is a reality. It is an opinion shared by ninety per cent of the population and there is some support for its reality in the criticisms of Scripture.

So, if these psychic gifts do exist, who is handing them out? Who or what is behind the phenomena?

13

Whose Gifts?

The Thalidomide drug may once have been described as God's gift to expectant mothers. Today we know better. For a generation we have witnessed the tragic, though often heroic progress of those handicapped by its use. They were often born limbless because a pharmaceutical company failed to adequately test a product. The medical profession benefited from a cruel lesson. Other disciplines also learned to double-check. But para-psychologists continue to jump to unchecked conclusions.

Christian parapsychologists, almost without exception, view psychic phenomena as gifts of God's creation; as natural, say, as a talent for music or sport. The gifts are labelled 'good', though several dangerous side-effects are accepted. It is my belief that the psychic has been labelled prematurely, without sufficient testing, and with a reliance on hopeful speculation which is beyond reason.

The whole area is still a minefield of doubtful theories and hazardous hypotheses. The few known facts are dwarfed by a mountain of speculation. Parapsychology is still trying to answer questions it first began to ask seriously a century ago. We certainly need to continue our investigations; to advance ideas; to plumb the mysterious depths of the human psyche. But premature confidence in a little-known, ill-tested theory is not a suitable attitude for Christians who are urged to test all things. We desperately need to avoid making hasty judgements, especially when it comes to the most basic question of all: whose gifts are they?

A section of Christendom answers that question with a blunt, no-nonsense cry of 'Satan!'. The paranormal is automatically consigned to the demonic because it is not immediately biblical. As a consequence, there is a reluctance to even devote thinking time to this subject. This section of Christianity is just as guilty as the premature parapsychologists. One believes that the psychic is satanic while the other presupposes that the gifts come from God. All this, while the field is festooned with unanswered question marks! Some of the larger ones demonstrate the uncertainties.

1. Angels on assignment?

Billy Graham retells a Reader's Digest story of Dr SW Mitchell, a celebrated Philadelphia neurologist, who was awakened one bitter, snowy night by a little girl knocking at his door.[1] She wanted him to follow her and treat her sick mother. The doctor trekked through the driving snow behind the girl, and then left her downstairs to go and tend to the mother. Later, the doctor complimented the mother on the intelligence of her child. The woman looked at him strangely, and then said, 'My daughter died a month ago!' Seeing the doctor's uncomprehending expression, she added, 'Her shoes and coat are in the clothes closet.' Dr Mitchell opened the door to find a coat identical to the one the girl had been wearing. It was warm and dry and could not possibly have been out in the snow storm.

'Could the doctor have been called in the hour of desperate need by an angel who appeared as this woman's young daughter?' queries Mr Graham. He goes on to relate many other such stories, mainly involving apparitions on the mission field.

A Bible-based Christian will want to check this query against the ways in which God has worked in the past. He will soon find, for instance, the stranger in the furnace with Shadrach, Meshach and Abednego (Daniel 3), and even the Mount of Transfiguration when Moses and Elijah conversed with the transformed and glorified Jesus (Matthew 17:1–8). Our understanding of certain phenomena, it would seem, does have to allow for the possibility of God at work. It would, however, be totally wrong to assume that all apparitions are angels on assignment. There are other possibilities, as we shall see from other questions.

2. God-given ESP?

Canon J Stafford Wright, an evangelical scholar and former principal of Tyndale College, Bristol, believes that the psychic might be man's link with the rest of the animal world. There is, for instance, he writes, the telepathic spread of habit changes, such as tits learning to peck through milk-bottle tops. This habit apparently began in Southampton and rapidly spread nation-wide.[2] He agrees with renowned biologist Sir Alister Hardy that there is evidence of 'a general subconscious sharing of form and behaviour patterns – a sort of psychic blueprint.'[3] He believes that there seems to be extra-sensory perception (ESP) between spiders who spin similar webs from birth, and flocks of starlings that twist and turn at great speed without colliding. From this and other instances, Stafford Wright concludes that God has made ESP 'a part of animal existence'.

Extra-sensory perception, however, seems to be an over-grand, and possibly misleading title for what may simply be God's pre-programming of his animal kingdom. Innate robotic responses or patterns of rapid learning in animals may be nothing more than an extension of their basic instincts. In other words, their senses are natural and in no way 'extra'. They are the basic, inbuilt minimum for survival. The birds and spiders do what they do because they can do no other. They are programmed. Instinct, or an extension of it, does not automaticaly equate with ESP or the psychic.

However, it would be wrong to dismiss this line of thought without further investigation. It is true to say that man has lost much since the perfection of Adam. It is possible that there are abilities of mind and soul that have been lost. It is also conceivable that there are still natural laws which are still to be discovered and named. Parts of the paranormal (perhaps telepathy or precognition) may yet have normal explanations. It is wrong, however, to prejudge an issue on the basis of hopeful speculation. Far better to wait, and continue testing.

3. Miracles or psychic ability?

'God may use latent psychic tendencies,' writes Canon Stafford Wright, 'and draw them out for his purposes.'[4]

He goes on to suggest that the amazing abilities of, say, Jesus and Elisha were 'natural capacities' which God took and 'used to a profitable end'. Jesus practised levitation when he walked on water (Mark 6:45f) and Elisha's clairaudience enabled him to overhear the enemy's tactical talks before battle (2 Kings 6:8–12). The canon also sees a demonstration of hypnotism causing an 'unusual form of blindness' when the men of Sodom were unable to see the angels in Lot's house (Genesis 19:11).

The equating of the biblical gifts with psychic gifts is commonplace in such journals as *The Christian Parapsychologist* and *The Quarterly Review*, both from The Churches' Fellowship for Psychical and Spiritual Studies. Is this approach justified on the available evidence, or is it another premature presupposition without a true basis?

Most Christian parapsychologists accept this equation without serious question. Stafford Wright is the same, though his own reasoning, at one point, includes a contradiction. He implies that the psychic gifts are of a different order than other gifts, when he warns,

> It is unwise for the average psychic to try to increase psychic ability. Not only does it tend to concentrate on psychic inner experience at the expense of the spiritual, but it inflates one's pride in having some superhuman power that others do not possess, and it is only too easy to overstep the boundary between the neutral psychic and the evil occult. The safer and proper thing is to offer the psychic phenomena to God, either to remove or to use them.

Scripture encourages the Christian to seek the gifts of God and to develop them as good stewards (1 Corinthians 14:1 and Luke 19:11f). If the psychic gifts are of God, our duty is clear. We should develop them to the full. If they are not of God, then we are right to be wary.

Of course, there is yet another consideration. In a Christian world view which revolves around the battle of good and evil, could not the devil – known as the father of lies – cause the gifts of God to be aped? This certainly happened in the case of Moses and the Egyptian magicians (Exodus 7:8f). Moses' staff changed into a snake when Aaron threw it to the ground before Pharaoh. The Egyptian magicians did the same through their secret arts. However, the Bible implies that the magicians' tricks were inferior and poor copies, for 'Aaron's staff swallowed up their staffs' (Exodus 7:12). This poses a query.

4. Satan's counterfeit gifts?

Scripture states that the devil is 'Antichrist' (1 John 4:1f) and ever anxious to destroy (John 8:44). He is also the enemy of mankind (Matthew 13: 37–39) and an angel of light (2 Corinthians 11:14,15). Is it not then possible that Satan, in his opposition to Christ and man, and wishing to destroy all that God has given, could do so by appearing in a godly angelic light? Should we not therefore expect God's gifts to have their satanic counterpart?

From this point of view there is a remarkable parallel between the gifts of the Holy Spirit and those in the psychic realm. Each scriptural gift (Romans 12:6f; 1 Corinthians 12:7f; and Ephesians 4:11,12) seems to have its 'ape':

Prophecy . . . mediumship, clairvoyance, precognition.

Teaching . . . automatic writing and mediums.

Wisdom and leadership . . . spiritualism, mediums.

Word of knowledge . . . precognition, automatic writing, mediums.

Miraculous powers . . . divination, automatic writing, telepathy.

There are several points to note:

(a) Some of the above, such as mediumship and spiritualism, are banned by Scripture (Leviticus 20:6,7). It seems reasonable to assume, therefore, that they are unlikely to come from the Author of Scripture.

(b) The gifts of the Holy Spirit are always used to build up the body of Christ and 'prepare God's people for the work of Christian service' (Ephesians 4:12). Few, if any, of the psychic gifts could claim to do this. Rather, they tend to turn people in on themselves, which certainly makes the devil happy.

(c) The Spirit's gifts encourage, inspire and build up those who receive them, and benefit from their use. Why is it that the psychic gifts often cause apprehension and even fear? Why have I and many others had to minister encouragement to those who have been discouraged by the psychic? Why have they needed extensive spiritual counselling in a bid to reconstruct their disintegrating personalities?

(d) The Spirit's gifts guide and help. Why then do the psychic gifts often seem to tease, confuse and obstruct? What's the use, for instance, of alarming sixty-odd people with a preview of the Aberfan disaster without telling them where it is, when it is going to happen, or how they can help to stop it happening? Why should God give a gift like that? For what purpose? Would it not be more like Satan to shoot a dart into the dreams of an unsuspecting person, so that he foresees a plane crash without any hope of helping or saving the situation? The resulting fear and frustration would seem to be more in line with the mockery of the devil.

(e) Could Satan's plan be to belittle the miraculous element of Christianity by 'aping' it? Astral travel seems to mimic the sudden disappearance of Philip after baptising the Ethiopian eunuch and his reappearance at Azotus (Acts 8:39,40). It is even closer to Paul's description of the man who was caught up into the third heaven (2 Corinthians 12:2). There are psychic similarities to many Gospel events whether it be the dreams and visions of Zechariah (Luke 1 and 2); the foreknowledge of Elizabeth concerning Mary's baby (Luke 1); Jesus knowing what was in people's minds (Luke 11:17); or the predicative prophecies of Jesus (Luke 19:39–44). The list of similarities is too numerous for these pages.

Perhaps, in our ignorance, we should not dismiss this query too hastily. Satan, who lacks creative originality, can only take that which God has created and misuse it for his own purposes. This counterfeiter of creation is always happy to lead people away from the real Jesus Christ. He tried in vain to misdirect Christ himself in the wilderness (Matthew 4). When that failed, he set about misleading man's understanding of Jesus. Every heresy and man–made religion that has ever been invented presents a fractured picture of Jesus Christ. Presenting Jesus as a super-psychic seems to fall dangerously close to Satan's goal.

(f) The gifts of the Spirit come out of a living relationship with the Father. The psychic gifts appear to originate from no particular relationship, according to most of those to whom I have had to minister. Jesus had no power of himself, he only communicated and performed through that which was given to him in relationship with the Father (John 17:7f).

5. Christianity blurred?

Psychics such as Jeanne Dixon, the late Doris Stokes and my local professional clairvoyant all claimed that their gifts fell from heaven. My professional clairvoyant friend, who was once heading for the Christian mission field, said,

'I was always sorry I wasn't converted. But when I look back, I think it's this path that's been ploughed for me. Any other thing that I would do now, I think, would be a violation of God's will for my life. I really believe that.'

I asked her where she believed her clairvoyance came from.

'I have to believe that it comes from angels, or spirit beings.' She added to this her view of heaven. 'I don't think they're all up there sitting, glorifying God. That would be hell for me. I'm an active person. God's going to get me back to work . . . and I know exactly what I'm going to do. I'm going to come from the light, right through the abyss (hell or purgatory) to help people down here . . . . I love my daughter very much. There is no way that anybody is going to stop me helping her if I die tomorrow.'

Those on the fuzzy fringe of the psychic and Christianity are invariably governed by their feelings or experiences. The Bible is treated as one of many sources of faith, but many tend to dismiss the bits they dislike while embracing the more comforting sayings. The world's Jeanne Dixons have, for example, to explain away the numerous warnings about contacting the dead (Leviticus 19:31: 20:6,7 & 27; Deuteronomy 18:10,11; 1 Samuel 28:7,8; 2 Kings 23:24 and others). The professional clairvoyant also has to ignore the many scriptural bans on fortune–telling (1 Samuel 28:3; 2 Kings 21:6; Isaiah 8:19,20; Daniel 2:2 and others). They must also overlook Jesus' specific illustration of the barrier which prevents real contact between the spirit–world and earth (Luke 16:26f).

Most of all, psychics of a Christian hue overlook one major contradiction. How can an unchangeable God hand out in this age what he has forbidden in another age? It would seem we are left with a straightforward choice. Do we believe God's written word or the feelings and experiences of clairvoyants?

6. A Satanic attack on the church?

Scriptural authority, or rather the lack of it, is at the heart of the difficulties experienced, for example, by The Churches' Fellowship for Psychical and Spiritual Studies. The fellowship, founded in 1953, 'exists for the study of wider reaches of the paranormal and extra-sensory perception in their relation to the Christian faith'.[5]

On a personal level, I have to say that I found the fellowship's officials to be delightfully hospitable and to have a genuine love for God. They offered their time, effort and resources to me willingly, and were ever anxious to set before me their personal views of this highly experimental area. You might suspect that, so far, this is the old technique of flattery before flattening. This would be only partially true. The fellowship itself has an innate self-criticism which comes from wading in the quicksands of the psychic.

A major problem which the fellowship recognises among its 1,400 membership is the over-reliance on experience. Nearly all of them have joined through exposure to psychic phenomena. Often, the experience becomes the governing factor in their lives. They have this 'one thing I know' experience, and in an uncertain world everything else tends to be judged in the light of that experience.

This is partly the view of the fellowship's chairman, the Venerable Michael Perry, who is also Archdeacon of Durham and the editor of the Fellowship's *The Christian Parapsychologist*. The archdeacon – again a helpful and hospitable man with a great knowledge gleaned from more than thirty years' experience of the paranormal – has written two books on his subject, *Psychic Studies – A Christian View* and *Deliverance*.

In both he treats the Bible as an important contribution to present-day theology. Nevertheless, he feels at liberty to be his own final authority in judging which parts to accept and reject. It seems to me that he tries the Bible before the bar of his own mind rather than the other way around. This allows him, for instance, to speculate on the plausibility of a form of reincarnation, which enjoys a large following in the psychic, paganism and the occult. He writes:

> Instead of hell, God might consign the impenitent or spiritually immature or those ignorant of him to another round of earthly life. It would be like returning to resit an examination in which we have not done well enough to proceed to another level of our education.[6]

Michael Perry stresses that these are no more than speculations prefaced by 'perhaps' and 'I don't knows', and adds the caveat that they must be tested against the touchstone of a Christian understanding. Tested against the touchstone of Scripture, his speculations would reduce the Bible to the size of a slim paperback. Out would go Judgement Day, the separation of sheep from goats, wheat from tares, hell and punishment, the justice of God and his wrath. Man's free will would have to go as well, and we would be left with an unloving, gatecrashing dictator God who refuses to allow people to choose their own eternal destiny. This is a Gestapo God 'who has ways of making us repent'!

The archdeacon's view of Scripture is again highlighted in his dismissal of the occult warnings of Old Testament writers. He treats them as shortsighted, intolerant and abusive prophets.

> The Old Testament has a nice line in vituperation of other cultures and their beliefs when its writers suggest that non-Israelites worship, not the true God, but satyrs or he-goats or

demons .... Perhaps all we are here witnessing is a picturesque way of making a scornful reference to alien religion.[7]

And again . . .

Why were the prophets so dead set against mediumship? They knew the same kinds of altered states of consciousness – could they not recognise the mediums as their allies rather than their enemies?[8]

This liberal approach to Scripture is dealt with more fully in a later chapter. For the present, it is wise to remember that Jesus did not have Mr Perry's problem with the Old Testament. He accepted it as the word of God. Certainly Jesus refined it and filled out its theology, but he still accepted it as God-breathed rather than the confused and ill-considered thoughts of ignorant men.

This take-some-of-it-or-leave-some-of-it approach to Scripture is the main reason for the fuzziness between Christianity and some forms of the psychic. It leaves people with no authority by which to judge what is right or wrong. They consequently have to rely on their own doubtful experiences and their imperfect reasoning.

Conclusion

With so many unanswered questions, it is an unwise man who comes to a conclusion. We are faced with a fund of conflicting speculations. No drug company would ever con-template issuing a medicine which had so many unproven and untested facets to it. Even the Thalidomide formula mentioned at the beginning of this chapter was only released after rigorous testing, save in one tragic area. To change the metaphor, if airlines offered a similar speculative scenario, only fools would fly. To encourage people to voyage into the psychic seems about as responsible as the Wright brothers taking day-trippers on their first ever flight – without parachutes!

I think of one lady I am counselling as I write this. Mary is 40. She was raped in her teens, and is now highly strung, very sensitive, still single, and open to all kinds of suggestions. Premonitions have fascinated her for several years. Fear of the phenomenon is also present. What do I say to this woman? Should I tell her that all is well and that what she has comes from God? Should I then go on to tell her that she should develop these gifts which frighten her? Can I honestly reassure her that she will come to no harm in pursuing this phenomenon?

I find that I have to be honest with Mary and many others. I have to point out gently that her gifts have never helped her become a better human being. They have only increased her nervousness. I have to point out that she is wasting her life caught up in waiting for her thoughts and ideas to come true in reality. Many of her thoughts pass into oblivion, while the occasional thought comes true to life. Her confusion is great in not knowing which of her thoughts is predictive of the future. She knows this only after the event. How then am I to counsel Mary in her distress and fascination?

I have no alternative but to advise Mary, and others, to keep their feet firmly planted on the sure foundation of Christ's teachings in Scripture. And as I counsel, I need to stay alongside them to provide comfort, encouragement and guidance. In fact I can offer no better advice than that already given by Canon Stafford Wright. Avoid the temptation to develop it, and ask God to remove it. The canon did add an alternative: that we ask God to control it. This I omit. I am not in any area satisfied that the psychic gifts are of God. My personal preference, while awaiting further light, is to look in the opposite direction.

14
The Hell of Reincarnation

Mahatma Ghandi called reincarnation a 'burden too great to bear'. The countless millions of Hindus and Buddhists down the ages would agree with him. It is, however, their *karma*, and they believe that there is nothing that they can do about it. They are resigned to a monstrous tread-wheel of punishment for eternity, and their only salvation is via the meditation of yoga (or Zen, the Buddhist equivalent).

Eastern reincarnation is about dying and returning to earth in another form, either above or below your previous status, depending on how good or bad you have been in a previous life. If you are a woman, you have no chance of salvation for that is reserved only for men. A woman's only hope is to serve her menfolk and in so doing earn the reward of being reborn as one of them.

'The most foolish male,' according to an Eastern saying, 'is more intelligent than the most intelligent female.'

One branch of Hinduism slavishly follow their gurus – god men – who claim to reveal the shortest routes to salvation. These invariably involve a range of meditations to transcend the suffering of a wounded continent. The quick ways of salvation include walking around naked, or blindfolded, or drinking the urine of cows (the animal which symbolises the female divinity of Mother Earth and Mother

India). For the really dedicated, sex is banned. This is perhaps just as well for they also plaster their hair with cow dung. Having done all this, the Hindu believes he will still not escape the ever-grinding Wheel of Samsara (reincarnation). However, he hopes that these additional sufferings will increase his capacity to meditate away the hunger pangs, disease and further suffering. Some gurus maintain that meditation can make a hungry person a 'happy hungry person'.

Reincarnation paralyses the initiative of millions. Those imprisoned by it rarely strive for social improvements or justice, for that would then deprive people of their karma – a merciless law of consequences. The suffering is the consequence of a previous misspent life. If it is avoided in this life, it will only be piled on to the suffering of the next life. There is no escape from karma. The only help acceptable are hints on how to improve meditation. Only the guru can provide this!

These gurus have now come West, and millions of Europeans and Americans have accepted a revamped version of reincarnation. The very hell that has caused the grotesque sufferings and early deaths of countless millions has become an enduring part of sophisticated Western man. Some opinion polls reveal that one in four people believe in reincarnation. This grotesque philosophy which ignores the matchstick legs and distended bellies of starving children has now hit the streets of London, Birmingham and Manchester. In the small Lancashire town where I minister, reputed to be a decade or so behind the times, twenty two per cent accept reincarnation in one form or another.

The gurus, emigrating to the West, have introduced their philosophies with a calculated sensitivity to European and American cultures. They travel in their own planes, helicopters and Rolls-Royces to bring modern man a modern doctrine of reincarnation. There is, for instance, no distinction between male and female, as in the East. There is no mention of the grinding agony of Samsara, nor that reincarnation is the nearest version of a hell-like punishment man can ever experience this side of the real thing.

The gurus' philosophy is clothed with scientific terminology and hailed as the missing link of evolution. New Agers take on board the idea of 'conscious evolution', one of the main Western names for reincarnation. This, we are told, is the way to reach the next stage in our development. Conscious evolution is the road to Utopia and a higher level of existence. It is that which will ultimately make us one with the divine, or the Masters, or the higher beings from outer space who have been guiding our planet through the dark eons on earth.

This form of reincarnation is sold in the West as another chance to make good; the way to true salvation, to greater knowledge and enlightenment.

'We do not just reincarnate as an individual soul into a new body each time,' says Graham Wilson, the founder-director of New Life Designs 'but more as a collective consciousness of souls, which is why we have access to a lot more information than we realise.'[1]

The Aetherius Society, which claims to have received its teachings from the Cosmic Masters while their founder, Sir George King, was in a positive Yogic Samadhic trance, is more honest about the true view of reincarnation.

'People have lived thousands of lives as people before and they will live endless more lives,' the society leaflet states. 'Much as each day follows the other in one's life, so does each life follow the previous life and is determined by one's conduct in previous lives. We are given endless opportunities to learn and evolve.'[2]

Resurrection

Christian resurrection is the antidote to reincarnation. Man lives one life and after that comes resurrection and judgement

(Hebrews 6:2 and 9:27). Jesus himself had to cope with those who denied a resurrection, in the form of the Sadducees. He told them, with patience and love, that they were in error because they did not know the Scriptures (Matthew 22:23–32). Jesus said that he was the resurrection (John 11:25) and he told his followers that he was going ahead of them to prepare a place for them (John 14:2). This did not entail an endless cycle of future lives. It is stressed that Jesus came once, for all (Hebrews 9:26).

There are two reasons why reincarnation is the fastest growing single philosophy in the West today. First, the church has failed miserably to get over the good news of true salvation in the death and resurrection of Jesus Christ. We have mislaid the truth that the sacrifice of Calvary has paid the penalty of man's sin once and for all (Romans 6:10); that nothing we can do can bring us nearer to salvation and God (Ephesians 2:8,9) – not if we tried for a million lifetimes. Secondly, man in his ignorance, and sometimes deliberately, has looked to others for hope and help. Resurrection means that life is a once-for-all-time experience and for those not willing to trust in Christ for salvation the future is exceedingly bleak. Upward evolution through several lives seems much more attractive to the person who knows himself to be a sinner and not worthy of saving. Another chance in another life is hard to resist, especially if he can put off the moment when he must repent and change his ways. After all, we are basically a selfish race and we love to go our own way and be our own gods. Thank God that God is not as selfish.

> For God so loved the world that he gave his one and only Son, that whoever believes in him shall not perish but have eternal life. For God did not send his Son into the world to condemn the world, but to save the world through him. Whoever believes in him is not condemned, but whoever does not believe stands condemned already because he has not believed in the name of God's one and only Son (John 3:16–18).

15
The Book That's Right

We had lost the map – and our way! We drove off the hovercraft at Calais, heading for Lille in Northern France. The town of Armentières and a contradictory signpost was our downfall. We ended up crossing into Belgium five times, much to the amusement of the border officials. My return smiles were becoming increasingly stifled by a rising panic, after being at the wheel of a minibus of weary teenagers for the previous eight hours.

I suspect a similar feeling is shared by millions in a world which has lost its directions. The journey of life is punctuated with unsignposted crossroads, unpredictable diversions and complex spaghetti junctions. At each inter-section stand the gurus, modern messiahs, occultists, pagans, liberal theologians and the Bible-believing Christians. Who is to be believed? Do any of them know the real truth and the way? By what authority do they beckon and direct the traveller – you and me?

The Bible, still the world's bestseller, was our nation's authority for 1800 years. Then came the attacks. Now we are told that it is only one of several maps with which to find our way. However, there still exists the mass of evidence to show that the Bible continues to be the best lamp to guide our steps and the only true light to illuminate our path through an often dark, confusing world (Psalms 119:105). For those who wish to pursue the evidence further than I can take it in a short chapter, a selected bibliography is added at the end.

Reasons to trust the Bible

1. It gets the future right. Divination plays a vital role in paganism and the occult. Most want to know what the future holds, and one of the realities of the occult is that there is no perfect system. Some would sell their souls for a window on fate. Television prophets of astrology make a fortune out of getting only 10% of their forecasts right. Other more dedicated occultists, like Jeanne Dixon and our stock-market wizards of Chapter 5, have more success, but even they are wrong more than they are right.

What then of the hundreds of predictive prophecies in the Bible? So far it has a 100% accuracy record! Not one prediction has failed. The only predictions which have not been realised so far are those to do with the end of the world. The biblical predictions include more than 300 concerning the life of Jesus. Imagine trying to guess the winners of the next 300 horse races in Britain! Then multiply those odds by a few thousand. Many of the prophecies were so outlandish that an Old Testament 'bookie' would have offered odds of a million to one against some of them happening. To insist that the Old Testament writers guessed everything correctly is stretching credulity to the outer limits. It requires less faith to believe that God inspired the writers and gave them the right information.

2. It gets the facts right. Humanly speaking, you would expect the Bible to be a book of its times. It should reflect no more than the limited knowledge of the times in which it was written. After all, every ancient book that has ever been penned contains errors in the light of modern discoveries. The Bible should be no different. It must be said that the

Bible does have a few odd descriptions, but these are largely restricted to its poetic sections, and poets of every age are allowed a certain licence in their use of picture words and phrases. The Bible is unique among ancient literature because of its remarkable accuracy in its historical and scientific facts.

From a historical point of view, Josh McDowell cites 'The Tables of Nations' in Genesis 10.[1] This is unique among ancient writings for its accuracy. Again, the five centuries of history from the beginning of 1 Samuel through to the end of 2 Chronicles score ten out of ten.[2]

From a scientific point of view, accuracy is the main feature, whether it concerns embryology, hygiene, agriculture, biology, astronomy, or whatever discipline. Scripture correctly insists, for instance, that there are as many stars as there are grains of sand on the seashore, despite the fact that the wise men of the day believed that there were only a few hundred.[3]

Archaeological discoveries also show that the Bible gets its facts right. Many scholars are today giving greater respect to Old Testament stories for no other reason than that the archaeological evidence demands it. That was the view of Professor H H Rowley. Renowned Jewish archaeologist Nelson Glueck wrote, 'It may be stated categorically that no archaeological discovery has ever controverted a biblical reference.'

The question arises: when every other ancient book is inaccurate in the light of later discoveries, how has the Bible managed to achieve scientific accuracy centuries before modern science itself was established? Is it really all outrageous guesswork? It seems much easier to believe that the writers were inspired and guided by Somebody in the know?

3. Jesus says the Bible gets it right. Jesus treated the Old Testament as the written word of his Father. The living Word of God accepted without question the written word of the Old Testament. He did not treat it as legend or myth. He quoted from all but eight of the Old Testament books and accepted them in the normal way that we understand words. He was quite happy to acknowledge that his whole purpose in coming to earth was to fulfil what had been written so far in Scripture. If Christ accepted the Old Testament as genuine, who am I to argue?

4. The writers get it right. Scripture comes to us via the minds and personalities of more than forty writers. It has two main divisions, many sub-divisions and contains sixty-six separate books. It was written over forty generations lasting 1500 years, on three continents and in three languages. It is also written in many forms of literature. Despite all this, there is a sensible theme running consistently from Genesis to Revelation. Every section is in line with a perfect creation, the fall of man, his multiplication, the flood, a new beginning, further degeneration, God's prophetic warnings, his dealing with his special people, God's salvation through his Son, a new strength and Spirit to follow him, the return of Christ and finally a new heaven and earth.

The occultist needs to pause for thought here. It might help him note the consistency of what forty-odd biblical writers received, and then compare it with the jumble of conflicting theories received by his own 'ancients'. Some occult writers claim inspiration. Others insist that they received their messages through automatic writing. Yet there is no agreement on the nature or character of the force, energy or whatever. It is not known if there is one force or many. There is a multitude of paths to reach the force or forces. Above all they do not even know whether or not they have got the truth, nor even if truth can be known.

The Bible is also relevant to today. It describes man – his condition, his strengths and weaknesses, and his environment – in down-to-earth practical language. Though written centuries ago, its principles and truths are as up-to-date as the latest 'hi-tech' science manual.

This book makes sense of life. It also makes sense that Somebody in charge must have been guiding the writers, spread out as they were over centuries, generations, continents and languages.

Pagans, occultists and liberal churchmen have one thing in common: they prefer to reduce the Bible, especially the Gospels, to nothing more than legend. Perhaps that is a little unfair on some of the occultists who actually accept the miraculous, such as the Virgin Birth and the Resurrection. In general, however, all parties believe that the Gospel writers were sincere men who used an honest way of writing called myth. The idea of myth is originally based on the idea that the stories of the New Testament circulated by word of mouth for many years before being committed to parchment. As the stories circulated, the pro-myth lobby claim that the historical facts were set aside and legends were formed. Rudolph Bultmann was the main modern thinker behind this trend.

The writers of the New Testament, however, could not disagree more. Paul stated that he was passing on to the Corinthians what was of the greatest importance! Christ had died and had risen again. Paul, writing twenty years after the event, implied that if any of his readers doubted the resurrection, then they could go and interview some of the five hundred followers who had seen Jesus alive and well after his death and burial (1 Corinthians 15:6f).

Luke, that most meticulous of doctors who always checked his facts, reported that the risen Christ went to great lengths to show his disciples that he was flesh and bone. This was no imagined appearance, no mere subjective 'resurrection experience'. This was the real thing; the real Jesus who sat down to a meal of cooked fish (Luke 24:36–43). The writer of 2 Peter assured his readers that he had not depended on 'made-up' stories. He had obviously met the forerunners of Mr Bultmann.

These New Testament writers were either deliberate liars

or they were writing the truth. Liars do not generally take to the streets and suffer torture and agonising deaths in defence of their lies! There is also much that is questionable about the ideas of the pro–myth parties. Normaly, myth takes many centuries to develop and has never been known to survive on such a scale as the gospels while witnesses to the actual events were still living.

It is interesting to note that non–Christian writers of the first century did not contradict the basic elements of the gospel. Any one of them would have been delighted to record the remotest suggestion of 'make-believe' or myth. But they did not!

Liberals and occultists insist that there are discrepancies in Scripture, but these criticisms are often crude and over-simplified. Very often they fail to take into consideration the intentions of the writers and unfairly criticise them for not doing what they in no way set out to do. John Stott wrote of the gospel writers and their intentions,

> It is possible to condense speeches, paraphrase them, and translate them into a different cultural idiom, without thereby falsifying their meaning; to change the sequence of events, deliberately subordinating chronology to theology, without this practice committing an error; to give round figures and make free quotations, according to the literary conventions of the pre-computer age, without being accused of making mistakes (imprecision is not a synonym for inaccuracy); and to quote the Old Testament in such a way as to draw attention to the principle, parallel or pattern, rather than the detailed fulfilment of a specific prophecy, without being guilty of misquotation.[5]

5. The Bible claims to be right. Most of the authors claimed that what they were writing was inspired by God; not once, but thousands of times. 'Thus says the Lord. . . ' they kept insisting.

'Well, they would, wouldn't they?' one witch scoffed as we talked about authority. The witch missed the obvious point. Writers who were liars might certainly claim God's inspiration, but what could they possibly gain by including graphic accounts of their own shameful faults? That would be the last thing a fraud would do. On the other hand, it would be the first action of an honest writer!

What about the Bible's morality? If the writers were liars, then they were the greatest con-artists in history. Why would they endlessly dwell on truth and justice, morality and righteousness for page after page? How could the world's greatest crooks conjure up the world's most precious moral teaching? And for what purpose? There are just too many unanswered questions if we treat the writers as liars. Centuries of civilisations accepted them as truthful. They recognised the Bible's teachings to be the pure gold of morality and righteousness, and were even prepared to build upon them.

The apparent contradictions in the gospels have convinced many of their authenticity. Fraudulent writers, intent on manufacturing a new religion for the gullible, would have done a much better job of getting their 'act' together. In my court reporting days before I became a minister, collusion between witnesses could be detected by the 'sameness' of their testimony. It was so obvious that they had got together beforehand and compared notes. Real-life court evidence always includes variations, because witnesses see things from different perspectives. The job of a court is to question and probe to see whether or not the differing accounts can be harmonised. It is the same with the gospels.

'A forgery would appear flawless *until* examination: the Bible becomes flawless only *on* examinaton.'[5]

6. The Bible is infinitely right. Dr D Martyn Lloyd-Jones, one of this century's foremost Bible expositors, preached for forty years and said on retiring that he felt he was only then beginning to understand the book. Great theologians have struggled to comprehend the breadth and depth of the Bible but with only limited success.

The finite human mind cannot embrace it. How then could a finite mind produce it? It can only have come from a mind that stretched to, and included, the infinite.

Consider also those who search for the infinite. Inevitably, as they seek God, they are drawn to the Bible. A yearning for God is always accompanied by a yearning to understand the Scriptures. Even the more honest seekers of the occult find this to be so. Many of them are like the Ethiopian eunuch, trundling through the wilderness and searching the Scriptures (Acts 8:26f). They read the Bible but are lost for want of a 'Philip' to give them some direction. God sent his disciple to interpret his book.

Scripture makes sense of the infinite. Witches, pagans, magicians, sorcerers, clairvoyants, and paranormal experts delve into their ancient mystery writings and find confusion. Few of them can agree. All occult systems have their own gods, or symbols or personifications. They confess themselves in ignorance, always striving for illumination. They walk in darkness and the light that their ancient writings provide has not overcome it. Their combined wisdom just does not make sense.

Conclusion

The case for the Bible's defence must rest, but only due to lack of space. We could devote several volumes to the archaeological finds which have substantiated many parts of Scripture. We could examine the hundreds of counterfeit sects based loosely on Scripture, and argue that imitation underlines the value of the original. It would be interesting to look at the logic of expecting a clearly written book from a God who loves his creatures and wants to help them. We could look at modern biblical criticism, acknowledge its positive contributions to our understanding of the Bible, and then move on to its destructive negatives and reveal the dereliction of its shaky foundations on ever shifting sand.

We could enter into a hundred and one other theological conundrums and use up the library shelves of the world with our output. It would be difficult to write that about any other book in history. But the case for the defence must rest. If this has whetted your appetite, then go on to one of the following:

Further reading

Josh McDowell, *Evidence That Demands a Verdict* (Here's Life Publications 1973).
J I Packer, *Under God's Word* and *Fundamentalism and the Word of God* (Lakeland 1980).
John R W Stott, *Understanding the Bible* (Scripture Union 1972).
D Martyn Lloyd-Jones, *Authority*.
F F Bruce, *Are the New Testament Documents Reliable?* (NP 1943).

16

How Christians Can Help

Two words should sum up the Christian's approach to all areas of the occult: *care* and *prayer*. Without care (both the loving and cautious aspects of the word) we can do more harm than good. Without prayer, we can do no good at all.

Now to the practical dos and don'ts.

1. Don't go solo. Jesus did not despatch his followers two by two without good reason (Luke 10:1f). The partnership was itself an encouragement, and they returned with great joy saying, 'Even the demons obeyed us.' Paul nearly always took a companion with him on his missions. We need to go and do likewise, especially when going into spiritual battle. Occasionally, this is not practicable, perhaps when talking with friends or family involved in soft-occult. In this case, recruit prayer support, even if it means breaking off for a quick telephone call.

2. Don't be off-putting. Staggering to the doorstep under your voluminous, chain-reference, floppy-leather Bible may frighten your host more than his occult experience! Use a less-threatening pocket-edition. Your clothes may seem irrelevant, but not if you visit a casual New Ager in your Sunday best. Equally, well-worn jeans and last week's tee-shirt are not guaranteed to endear you to the high-class lady spiritualist you have come to help.

3. Don't flounder. In fact, do not get involved if you know a particular ministry may be beyond your knowledge and experience. Realise that the occult is almost as far-reaching as the truth of God that it tries to ape. Call on others who have experience, especially if it involves the hard occult. Even the apostles wondered why they were unable to cope on occasions (Matthew 17:16). When unavoidably thrust into a counselling situation, a hasty but silent conference with the Lord will do wonders. It is, however, often better to return at a future time with somebody who knows what they are doing.

4. Do take notes. The Holy Spirit does give discernment but this needs to be supported by as much information as is practical. We need to discipline our own feelings and find out the following before making any judgements: name and address of person, age, marital status, family relationships, church background, any known family involvement with the occult (ouija, spiritualism, tarot, astrology, freemasonry, eastern practices, etc), state of person's health (hints of history of mental illness or depression; sexual orientation and views; physical condition; present or past medication; sleep; worries), person's job or lack of it, and finally the history of the house and neighbourhood. It is generally not a good idea to pull out a reporter's note-pad and pen at the beginning of an interview. On occasions it will seem right to jot down notes on a spare scrap of paper. Otherwise, commit the facts to memory and make the notes as soon as possible after your chat.

5. Do listen. Securing the above information helps the counsellor to use his most effective tools – the ears. There is nothing more irritating than a counsellor who is too anxious to counsel. It is akin to the GP writing out a prescription before you have had chance to sit down. Jumping to con-clusions should be left to suicidal kangaroos! There will be enough obstacles to honest talk without the counsellor adding any.

6. *Don't overlook drugs*. Alcohol and drugs are often involved. The greatest difficulty is discerning whether the presenting symptoms (hallucinations, fears etc) are caused by drugs, or whether the drugs have made a person more susceptible to spiritual attack. Frequently, it can be a combination, with one influencing the other. Recently a young woman, a known drug-pusher, told of awaking to see a strange dark figure, and later finding an 'A' mark scratched on the inside thigh of her toddler. There was evidence she had been taking magic mushrooms in the week leading up to her visit. Is it spirit-induced or plain child abuse? Support and care is being given, but action waits for more understanding.

7. *Do keep confidences*. Beware of Christian gossip under the guise of 'sharing a prayer topic'. By all means recruit prayer support, but retain anonymity. Beware especially of the Press. The occult provides high-readership copy and normally distorts and sensationalises. My local evening paper succeeded in distracting readers from a price rise by using a series on the occult. That is how much they value this news topic.

8. *Do be sensitive*. You have been invited into a person's life. Consequently, remember whose territory you are on. Do not gatecrash beyond the level you have been made welcome. Wait for the invitation to go further and deeper. If you need to ask more personal questions, ask your host's permission. Good manners cost nothing, and the opposite may lose you everything. Above all avoid gasping! You may have sufficient cause, especially if you are new to the occult. There are beliefs beyond belief and practices which make you feel dirty just to listen to them. Try to retain a calm, objective manner, while at the same time being relaxed and open. If you can do that while all around you is the rottenness of the occult, then praise the Lord for his help. Showing alarm can lead to one of two problems. Firstly, the introvert person will stop talking, fearing your revulsion and

alarm. Secondly, the extrovert character may be tempted to pour on the agony with even greater revelations, and may even start to delight in your discomfort.

9. Do avoid criticism. Backbiting and bitchiness have reached epidemic proportions in some areas of the occult, especially witchcraft and satanism. If we are over-negative in our criticisms, it may give the impression that Christianity is the same. It is especially never a good practice to attempt character assassination of some occult founder or leader. Remember that our early Christian leaders were no angels and nor are we. Certainly we need to point out errors, but with a generous amount of Christian love and with no thought of scoring debating points. We need to stress the positive gifts of our almighty Saviour. The offer of joy, peace, security, and the victorious power of the Holy Spirit will be the best antidote to the backbiting that may have been encountered in the past.

10. Do expect criticism. The rumour had apparently run rife through the town before a complete stranger let us in on the secret.

'Are you and your wife really witches?' a mother asked after inquiring whether or not I would baptise her child.

'I think you'd better come to church a few times and find out,' I smiled, trying to use the rumour to the best advantage. 'If you still think I'm a witch after a few weeks, we'll have another chat.'

On another occasion, a satanist leader circulated the rumour through his temple congregation that I had married my wife for her money. This provided us with a smile and a new twist to a family joke. My wife had always accused me of marrying her for her piano!

The criticisms can sometimes be nearer the truth and more serious. We need to understand the forces which affect the people with whom we are dealing. Love them and aim your resentment at the devil within.

11. Don't manufacture demons. Investigate all normal

explanations before turning to the occult. In many cases, we will not have to go any further. Do not assume that a person is demonised because he or she has dabbled with ouija boards or tarot cards. People can dabble in Christianity and remain completely detached from the Holy Spirit. Surprisingly, people can actually escape possession and even oppression though they may have attended or been involved in satanism. In all cases, though, it is good to get such people to renounce their involvement at the earliest opportunity.

12. Do act when necessary. We can be over-cautious and freeze, especially when we read or hear of deliverance ministries that have gone tragically wrong. If you have discounted reasonable doubts and you are sure that a person is demonised or affected by the occult in some way, then do something about it. If you do not feel adequate, enlist the help of those more experienced and proficient.

13. Don't discount anger. There is a place for controlled righteous anger in ministry to those affected by the devil's tricks. The anger should never, of course, be directed at the affected person, only that which is influencing him. In the original Greek of Mark 1:25 there is a stern seething hatred of evil as Jesus commands an evil spirit to 'be quiet' and to 'come out' of a man in a synagogue. Controlled anger can also encourage the counsellor in his authority over demons. As we exhibit the justifiable wrath of God, the demons shudder and flee. Care needs to be taken with anger, and that is why I have prefaced it with the word 'controlled'. After all, we do not want the affected person to shudder and flee!

14. Do be prepared. Firstly, we need to be filled with the Holy Spirit and sensitive to his leading. Close communion with the Lord ensures maximum distance between ourselves and the devil. The full armour of God carries a guarantee when worn according to the Maker's instructions. I can heartly recommend the practice of quick-fire telegram prayers when you are in the thick of a spiritual battle. Secondly, read up on your subject if you know that you are going to be involved in a counselling situation. A review of the material in this book and many of the other Christian publications I have mentioned will help your preparation. If you believe you have a ministry in this area, or will be forced by circumstances to exercise an extended ministry, then do get some training at a healing or counselling centre.

15. *Do avoid Christian charms.* The 'holy water and crucifix' brigade are rather better on the silver screen than in real-life ministry to the occult. Do not rely on any sacred article or substance, not even the Bible. The living contents in you should be your security. Having said that, it is true that 'sacred' items may be helpful if the person you are praying for has faith in them (see Acts 19:12).

16. *Do avoid dead ritual.* Prayer books, ceremonies and services need to have as much Holy Spirit power injected into them as possible, if used at all. I remember one formal baptism we had for a lady with a spiritualist background who came out of the service beaming from ear to ear. She had experienced a wonderful release from her past. However, our simple but commanding prayers can often be as powerful – or more so – as all the written liturgy in Christendom. When the Holy Spirit is given the use of our minds and tongues, he does not need anything else.

17. *Do be a spiritual realist.* Beware of either over- or under-estimating the devil and his forces. On the one hand, have confidence. When the Spirit of God is in residence in our lives, he puts up the 'no vacancy' sign. Evil spirits have no squatter's rights. Remember God's great promise through Paul, 'For I am convinced that neither *death* nor life, neither angels nor *demons*, neither the present nor the future, nor *any powers*, neither height, nor depth, nor anything else in all creation, will be able to separate us from the love of God that is in Christ Jesus our Lord.' (Romans 8:38,39).

On the other hand, acknowledge the dangers. Security in Christ can too easily become smugness in our own spirituality! The second a person realises he has become a spiritual giant is the precise moment he begins to lose his balance. And giants have the hardest of falls. Evil spirits might not be able to take possession of us, but they do have an uncanny knack of knowing when we have left one of our spiritual 'skylights' open. Christians can become affected, for no Christian has perfected the complete indwelling of the Holy Spirit. We leak too much for that to happen. If you do become affected, immediate confession, repentance and the counsel of mature Christians is the antidote. If you are forced to minister in the occult, ensure that you retain confidence in Christ, humility in yourself and a healthy appreciation of your foe.

18. Do avoid temptation. You are up against a clever adversary. If Eve, God's first perfect lady, fell, so may we. Serpents come in all shapes and sizes and most do not bare their fangs. I recall a Christian leader calling late at night with a rather anxious expression on his face. He asked if I could remember where he was on a certain evening at 8pm. It struck me as the strangest of requests, but I gave it some thought. I suddenly realised that I had been with him at that time for a long chat. Having said so, he asked whether or not I would be prepared to testify to that in court. A woman he had been counselling had apparently accused him of a sexual offence at the time of our chat. Fortunately, he had a water-tight alibi. The moral of the tale is obvious. Even if you go with a partner, take care not to get separated for too long. Compromising situations are an ever-present danger for the counsellor, especially in the occult, and blackmail is always a possibility.

It might seem a strange warning, but refuse any suggestions of having your photograph taken! This year alone, occultists have asked three times if I would mind if they took a 'snap-shot'. When one considers how they use photographs in place of voodoo dolls, and images in sympathetic magic, it is best to say no. Whatever they do to a photograph will not harm a Christian protected by the Holy Spirit, but it can give them further encouragement and temptation to go on dabbling.

19. Do expect retaliation. Anonymous threats by post or telephone are common among those involved in ministry to the occult. It may be a comfort to know that I have no knowledge of any threats ever having been acted upon either with myself or others. I have always followed the practice of burning everything I have received, whether they be letters, tapes, photographs or occult paraphernalia. Whatever you receive will probably have been 'powered' during occult rituals, before being dispatched to do their damage. Treat yourself to a back-garden bonfire if you do not have an open fire at home.

20. Do offer fellowship. This is possibly one of the hardest parts of any ministry. The prayer of deliverance is only the beginning. Follow-up counselling and generous portions of encouragement in a loving Christian fellowship are vital. Remember, an evil spirit may have been evicted but it may return with reinforcements if the treated person is left undefended (Matthew 12:43f). He may need to be won over by love to accept the loving Christ into his life. Be prepared for disappointment at this stage. A troubled person can easily reject your Christian overtures once he feels he is back to normal. More often, a released person will be so grateful and impressed by the power of our God that he will want to get to know him better. Beware that you do not turn him into one of your spiritual 'scalps'. Try and ensure that people in your felowship do not look on him as a 'prize' or an oddity. Be welcoming, accepting and encouraging.

21. Don't be the entertainment. Many occultists enjoy a good theological debate, and are only too delighted to use you for their entertainment. Believer-baiting is one of their favourite diversions.

22. Do focus on essentials. We can get so easily side-tracked by dead-end discussions on the pros and cons of the Zodiac or some other trivial issue. The major issues are the identity and character of the real God as opposed to the false gods, cosmic masters, life-force or whatever; the authority on which we should stand (Scripture versus experience, feelings or ancient wisdom); and, most important of all, the identity and character of Jesus. You stand every chance of getting to the heart of the issues if you bring the discussion round to 'the way, the truth and the life'.

23. Do realise that demons are not always the root of the problem. More often than not spirits have gained access through a perversion, habit, or chronic state of sin. Look for the perversion. Ask the Holy Spirit to reveal this supernaturally, if it is not evident.

24. Do acknowledge that the perversion may not be the fault of the victim. Let us remember the logic of the spiritual inheritance. Blessings and curses do not stop at one generation. It is a foundational truth enshrined in the Ten Commandments that the sin of the fathers will affect the children to the third and fourth generation. So often this cause-and-effect chain rattles through centuries: incest begetting incest, hatred giving birth to hatred, and so on. There is such a thing as sin being dyed into the bloodline of a family. It is ancestral sin that goes on breeding, with each new generation following in the footsteps of father. As Christians, guided by a forgiving Father and having the power of the Holy Spirit, we need to recognise that even this generation's sin can be dealt with. Perhaps we should also acknowledge that people can be affected spiritually when they are the victims of sin. Think of the hatred and inner corruption that takes place in a victim of rape or incest.

25. Do not be afraid. This ministry of deliverance is no more to be feared than any other ministry. The fear level of Christians is more to do with the devil's work than with spiritual reality. He loves to see us run away from him and his works. This certainly happened with me nearly twenty years ago when, as an inexperienced Christian, I first became involved in the deliverance ministry. My introductory brush with the demonic scared me so much that I vowed never to go near this ministry again. We need to remember that the devil and his spiritual forces dislike a head-on confrontaton with Jesus' people. It is the devil's role to flee if we resist. Remember that great promise of Hebrews 13:5–6: 'Never will I leave you; never will I forsake you. So we say with confidence, The Lord is my helper; I will not be afraid.'

26. Do leave the door open. Your visit to those in the occult or paganism may not be a success. But ensure that your exit is. This may sound like good advice given to double-glazing salespeople, but in Christianity it is even more important. It is not simply a question of losing a sale, the person's soul is at stake. If you give vent to any feelings of anger and frustration, one thing is probable: neither you nor any other Christian will be able to return at a future date. Be encouraged if you have handled yourself in a sensitive and gentle manner. Realise that the hostility or rejection that you might have to suffer is aimed not at you personally but at God and the gospel.

NOTES

Acknowledgements

1. *To God Be the Glory*, published by Hyndburn Christian Fellowship.
2. Hyndburn Christian Fellowship is centred on Accrington in the shadow of Pendle Hill. It is a loose partnership of sixteen churches which linked with forty-eight other churches in North-east Lancashire during Mission England.
3. Geoffrey Dickens, MP for Littleborough and Saddleworth, is right to raise questions in the House, and I welcome them. Some of the information he used originated from this book in its manuscript form. I cannot, however, go with him in his campaign to outlaw witchcraft. The law has the sensitivity of a sledgehammer when dealing with deep emotions and strong beliefs. The law can also be blind. Legislate against witchcraft this year and next year somebody will want to outlaw Christianity. Let MPs protest. Let us ensure that when the law is broken there is action. But let us leave the law as it stands. The days of inquisitions are, thankfully, long past.

Chapter 1

1. I merely state the two facts of the witch's curse and his subsequent death. I have no idea if there is a causal connection. I do know that my family and I have been conscious always of God's victory and protection. A neighbouring colleague, who was instrumental in a local witch's conversion to Christ, explained that the woman had confessed attempts to place a curse on his family but was unable to do so because the power of God was greater.

2. Chairman's Letter, Summer 1987, *Quarterly Review of the CFPSS*, p.3.

3. Other sites included Japan's Mount Fuji; Ayres Rock, Australia; Peru's Inca city of Macchu Picchu; California's Mount Shastra; and the Great Pyramid in Egypt. The international gatherings were part of what was called an 'Harmonic Convergence'.

4. The international press carried adverts declaring that Christ had come to earth on April 25th 1982, and again since. He is the Lord Maitreya. Benjamin Creme, an elderly English esotericist, claims to be the one who is preparing the way. (See Constance Cumbey, *Hidden Dangers of the Rainbow*, Huntington House 1983, in the Preface.)

5. Shirley MacLaine, *Out on a Limb* (Bantam Books 1983), p.209.

6. *Danger: Children at Play*, Evangelical Alliance, largely based on research by David Porter. See also David Porter's instructive book *Children at Risk* (Kingsway 1986).

7. National opinion poll for Channel 4 programme *Is Anybody There*, conducted by Surrey University, October 31st 1987.

Chapter 2

1. SAS and SOE information from Charles Fraser Smith with Kevin Logan, *Secret Warriors* (Paternoster Press 1984).

2. Courtesy of William Blake's *Jerusalem*. It must be the only poem which poses questions the answers to which are 'no' every time! My apologies to Blake for transposing 'mills' to 'hills'.

3. David Gardiner, *Trumpet Sounds for Britain*, Vol.1.

4. Many occultists claim that the church itself is to blame for the devil's barbed tail and horns. They maintain that the church could not make the natives forget their old gods, so it took the path of least resistance by incorporating them as the demons in the new religion. One said, 'Don't blame the devil when the church shoots itself in the foot!' There is an element of truth in this. Early Christians wrote of pagan gods as devils, and some of the gods were depicted as horned animals with tails and cloven hooves, like Pan. Thus the devil earned his characteristics. Artists and writers reinforced this caricature. Scottish poet Robert Burns referred to Satan as 'Auld Hornie' and 'Clootie'. This, of course, is not to deny the real existence of the devil and his forces. The Christian church merely acknowledged that the pagan gods were of the devil.

5. Retired minister the Rev Percy Nuttall used his life savings to purchase a disused Baptist chapel near Burnley, Lancashire, after a Manchester high priestess tried to buy it for use as a temple. The chapel is now run as a residential Christian holiday and conference centre. Percy did not live to see the realisation of his project. He died suddenly from heart failure the week before it opened. The local press carried the high priestess's boast that her curse was responsible. The truth was more likely that the lord called home 73-year-old Percy for a good rest after a job well done. See note 1, page 198.

6. Wicca, according to witches who follow Gardiner, is the name of the old pagan religion of Britain. They maintain that it is a saxon word meaning 'the craft of the wise', or 'the wise ones'. Other occultists believe it is derived from the Anglo–Saxon word 'wice' meaning 'wicked!' Modern wiccans apparently prefer to ignore this alternative. Some believe that 'wicca' dates back to the immediate post-war years, and was invented by modern writers on witchcraft.

7. From the price list of The Sorcerer's Apprentice, Leeds.

8. The Qabbala (also Cabbalah, Qabalah and Kabbalah) literally means 'from mouth to ear', an oral tradition of Jewish legends allegedly given to Abraham by God. It has no reputable authentic link with historical Judaism, but nevertheless has been a major influence on European magicians and their thinking.

9. *'Danger: Children at Play'*, Evangelical Alliance.

10. The EA leaflet is accurate, but the quoted book is inaccurate in its description of a 'Black Mass', according to Husyman, *La Bas* and Rhodes, *The Satanic Mass*.

11. *Sunday Express* and colour supplement, June 14th 1987.

12. *Q.E.D.* on television advertising, BBC 2, April 13 1988

13. Advertisement in *Accrington Observer & Times*, Nov 10th 1985.

Chapter 3

1. Dom Robert Petitpierre, OSB (ed.), *Exorcism* (SPCK, 1972).

2. Michael Green, *I Believe in Satan's Downfall* (Hodder & Stoughton 1981) p.20.

3. Statistics from the Government's Office of Population Censuses and Surveys as of September 1987.

4. Philosopher Ralph Waldo Emerson Jnr.

5. A familiar spirit is normally a spirit who controls a medium. It is likely that 'familiar' refers to knowing things by supernatural means. In the occult, a familiar

is a spirit-aid for witches and magicians (often, it is claimed, in the guise of a cat or dog). Witchcraft lore suggests that the 'familiar' is the devil's personal gift to his disciple.

6. Elemental spirits (also translated as 'principles' or 'ruling spirits') could mean ungodly angels, as used in Galatians 4:3 or even false gods as implied in verses 8–9. The word in other literature is also used to refer to component parts of our human make-up.

7. J Stafford Wright, *Christianity and the Occult* (Scripture Union 1971) p.50.

Chapter 4

1. Don Brothwell, *The Bogman and the Archeology of the People* (British Museum Publications 1986), p.32.

2. Ibid.

3. Whether or not these 'wise ones' were the original wiccans (see Chapter 2, Note 6), is uncertain. The late Dr Margaret Murray put forward this theory in her writings, but it has now fallen into disrepute among occultists. What is probable is that the secrets of magic and paganism were known by certain individuals in tribes and villages, and passed on to their successors.

4. This is not to imply that modern pagans indulge in orgies. A number do use the occult as an excuse for sexual pleasure, and more serious occultists use sex magic in their rituals. The dedicated occultist frowns on the excessive use of sex magic because of the inherent problem of enjoyment. They find that this different sort of magic takes their minds off the aim of real magic. The climactic emotion of sex is one of many that an occultist will use to 'catapult' his spell from his mind to where he wants it to do its work. Fear is another 'trigger' emotion. One occultist spoke of using the terrifying 'Revolution' ride at Blackpool's fun fair to release his

spells. He would use the terror of the upside-down ride to propel his magic.

Chapter 5

1. Dragon's Blood is a herb. In addition to staining, occultists use it in performing their own exorcisms.

2. Goetic Theurgy is recognised as one of the most lethal paths of magic and involves calling up an ancient god of the magician's choice. The magician's aim is to merge with the god's personality for the purpose of 'recording' all its knowledge, and then using that knowledge to his own advantage. Occultists treat Goetic Theurgy with great reverence, and are warned that they will have to pay a heavy cost if they abuse the gods. Some treat the gods as actual reality, but most believe them to be the symbolic manifestations of the occult forces. During the rituals the magician, in an altered state of consciousness, 'travels' to astral planes and is warned that he can be attacked and beaten up by the lower forces or spirits if he has not performed with the proper safeguards and knowledge.

3. My children warn me that the 'Upside-Down Land' game originated from one of their books. If this is the case, my apologies to whomever the author might be.

4. R G Torrens, *The Golden Dawn*, p.9.

5. Ibid.

6. An Oxford don took this 'reality' argument to its logical conclusion when he wondered whether the tree in the college quad actually existed if nobody looked at it. The answer, of course, has to be yes. His ancestors would have known a time when the tree was not there. Even in the don's life time, the tree would have changed, and would be seen to change consistently by all sighted human beings. Its reality would be brought home when, at the end of the tree's life, a gust of wind toppled it on to the head of some other Oxford don, whether he was looking at it or not!

7. Yin and yang are known in Western Europe as T'ai Chi.
8. Michael Green, *op.cit.*, p.18.
9. J Stafford Wright, *The New Bible Dictionary* (IVP 1962), p.766.
10. The occultist claims the Christian operates double-standards by applauding Moses' 'use of magic' while criticising the imitations of the Egyptian magicians. Scripture makes it clear that Moses used the power of God whereas the magicians 'imitated' it with the use of forces in other ways. The Egyptians are correctly criticised for relying on their false gods or forces rather than on the one, true God.
11. Interview with Silvanus in 'Lucifer over Lancashire', BBC 2 *Open Space*, April 1987.
12. Interview with unnamed occultist in 'Lucifer over Lancashire' (see previous note).

Chapter 6

1. *Paths of Magic* tape, The Sorcerer's Apprentice, Leeds.
2. Ibid.
3. To be fair to occultists and pagans, many systems do have a well-developed code of ethics. Many claim to follow the Right-Hand Path (what some call white magic), which is the use of magic for the good of others and themselves. From the Christian perspective, however, the means does not justify the end, no matter how laudable the motives. The Bible always condemns magic as a means because it relies heavily on the worship of false gods or forces.
4. Alan D Gilbert, *The Making of Post-Christian Britain* (Longman 1980), p.75.
5. *The Chaosphere* tape, The Sorcerer's Apprentice, Leeds.
6. Shamanism originates from North-East Asia. Its central belief is that the 'spirits' can only be controlled and influenced by the shaman (priest or medicine man). Austin Spare refined parts of it for European use.

7. The study necessary to become an adept (one who is skilled) in the occult is equivalent to a four-year university honours degree course. it is said that the 'graduate' never stops learning.

8. Directions leaflet accompanying the *Paths of Magic* tape (see Note 1).

9. Silvanus interview in 'Lucifer over Lancashire' (see Chapter 5, Note 11).

10. An unnamed chaos magician in 'Lucifer over Lancashire' (see Chapter 5, Note 11).

11. The occult also recognises the Left–Hand Path. This is the way of the dark magician; the black magic path of destruction.

Chapter 7

1. A motorist without documents is given an HO/RT/1 form which requires presentation at a nominated police station within seven days.

2. The five-pointed star pentagram (also called pentalpha) symbolises many esoteric qualities and is one of the main identifying symbols of the occult.

3. Most research material on witchcraft criticises the use of young children's evidence against witches. The children's lack of education, and possible hysteria are mentioned. However, this must be set against modern English law which makes no distinction between evidence given by a minor and that of an adult, providing the court is satisfied that the child understands right from wrong and the meaning of the oath.

4. Physical torture was illegal. There are, however, suggestions that the Witch–finder General, Matthew Hopkins, used sleep deprivation to extract confessions from suspected witches.

5. Witches were not burnt at the stake in England. This form of execution in England was reserved for treason.

6. Sabbat, probably a corruption of sabbath, is a weekly

convention of witches. It seems to have emerged as a word at the beginning of the persecutions, and was probably coined not by the witches, but by the persecutors.

7. Ian Robinson, 'Lucifer over Lancashire' (see Chapter 5, Note 11).

8. Both men and women are referred to as witches. The male title of warlock ceased to be used centuries ago.

9. From a ritual in 'Lucifer over Lancashire' (see Chapter 5, Note 11).

10. God is not only transcendent (above and different from his creation) but also immanent (dwelling within and working in his creation Psalms 139:7–10; Jeremiah 23:23,24).

11. November 1987. This debate continued into 1988 and subsequent comments and disciplinary actions by individual bishops improved the church's ethical and theological stance on homosexuality.

Chapter 9

1. Caryl Matrisciana, *Gods of the New Age* (Harvest House 1985), book cover.

2. Constance Cumbey, *op.cit.*, fourth flyleaf.

3. Quoted in Roy Livesey, *Understanding Deception: New Age Teaching in the Church* (New Wine Press 1987), p.234.

4. Alice and Stephen Lawhead, *Pilgrim's Guide to the New Age*, (Lion Publishing 1986), back cover.

5. Martin Stott, *Spilling the Beans*, (Collins/Fontana 1986), p.8.

6. Those in the occult point out that science originated with the Greeks who were polytheistic. This of course is true, but it was a very limited body of knowledge with no overall reason and, consequently, no unifying logic. Until Isaac Newton, science was an indisciplined infant which had little control over its functions. To be blunt, it was still in 'nappies'.

7. The 'Lucifer' company was later renamed 'Lucis', from the root words for 'light-bearer' and 'light' respectively.

8. Two-thirds of Britain's work force has already joined a part-cashless society with wages paid directly into the bank. In November 1987 a campaign was launched to persuade the other third to fall in line. Many social commentators are now wanting to remove cash from society to reduce muggings and wage-snatches. Mary Stewart Relfe Ph.D in her book *When Your Money Fails* warns of the collapse of the world's major currencies. Money, she reasons, will be replaced by Electronic Fund Transfer with each person having a single card and number. She outlines several experiments of placing a mark on the body, to replace plastic cards. She also highlights the worldwide usage of the Mark of the Beast – 666, the code for the World Banking system.

9. New Designs' tenth anniversary leaflet.

10. An inherited baronacy in 1958.

11. *The First Twelve Years*, Wrekin Trust guide, pp.4–5.

12. *The New Humanity Journal* June–July 1984, Year 10, No. 57, p.7.

13. Ibid, p.3.

Chapter 10

1. *Daily Mail*, November 20th 1987, p.6.

2. Italy's 'La Stampa' began publishing weekly horoscopes for dogs on September 25th 1987, to boost circulation.

3. Kurt Koch, *Between Christ and Satan* (Kregel Publications 1971), p.26.

4. John Allan, author of *Dealing with Darkness* (Handel Press 1986).

5. Fred Gettings, *Dictionary of the Occult* (Rider 1986), p.72.

Chapter 11

1. Peterborough Diocesan Magazine, Bishop William Westwood's Letter, June 1986.

2. Archbishop Robert Runcie's sermon, Whit Sunday 1986.
3. *Doorways to Danger*, Evangelical Alliance.
4. Adrian B. Smith (ed.), *TM: An Aid to Christian Growth* (Mayhew McCrimmon 1983), Epilogue, p.143.
5. Ibid, p.11.
6. Ibid, Introduction pp.11–20.
7. Ibid, p.38.
8. Ibid, p.124
9. Ibid, p.105
10. Ibid, p.34.
11. Ibid, p.132. The powers are called 'siddhis', the practitioner is a 'siddha'. The overall programme is known as 'The TM–Sidhi Programme' (spelling variations as given).
12. Ibid, p.125.
13. Patrick Sookhdeo, *Church of England Newspaper*, October 27th 1978.
14. *Paths of Magic* tape, The Sorcerer's Apprentice, Leeds.
15. Richard Littleman, *Yoga for Health* (Hamlyn 1971) based on ITV series, p.63.
16. Martin & Deidre Bobgan, *Hypnosis and the Christian* (Bethany House 1984), p.35.
17. Ibid p.22.
18. Dr Thomas Verny with John Kelly, *The Secret Life of the Unborn Child*, p.168.
19. Frank Lake, *Tight Corners in Pastoral Counselling*
20. Stephen Knight, *The Brotherhood* (Grafton 1985), pp.15, 16.
21. Lady Queensborough, *Occult Theocracy*, published 1933 after her death, pp.220–221.
22. *Freemasonry and Christianity – Grand Lodge's Evidence on Compatibility*, p.47.
23. *The Hermetic Order of the Golden Dawn* put the theory of the occult into practice and, in doing so, brought a revival of interest in esotericism. It began in London in

1877 to unravel the wisdom of the Ancients and to show how they could be applied in daily life.

24. John Symonds, *The Great Beast. The Life of Aleister Crowley*, p.22,24.

25. R G Torrens, *The Golden Dawn* p.11.

26. *The Great Beast*, p.118.

27. Ibid, p.119.

28. Maury Terry, *The Ultimate Evil* (Grafton 1987), back cover.

29. The Royal Arch is the completion of the 3rd degree Master Mason. The first two degrees are Entered Apprentice and Fellow Craft. Above the Royal Arch degree are thirty higher or side degrees, which are taken in groups of degrees on three occasions. The last three degrees have to be taken one at a time. Two-thirds of masons never go higher than Master Mason. The remaining third go on to the Royal Arch, but only a minority of those go to further degrees. From this point onwards, progress is by invitation only. The majority of ordinary Craft Masons (below Royal Arch) know little of what goes on above them. To each degree its own secrets.

30. Anglican Working Group report, p. 53.

31. For 250 years, Canon 2335 of Roman Catholicism brought automatic excommunication for members who became masons. In 1974, it was reinterpreted on softer lines and many Catholics became masons. The Congregation for the Doctrine of the Faith realised their blunder, and in 1983 declared that Catholic masons 'may not receive Holy Communion'. The Methodists in 1985 urged members to resign from the Craft and banned masonic meetings on church property. This was later softened. The General Synod of the Church of England in July 1987 accepted that there were 'a number of very fundamental reasons to question the compatibility of Freemasonry and Christianity'. Similar rulings had

previously been made by the Free Presbyterian Church of Scotland, the Reformed Presbyterian Church of Northern Ireland, and the Salvation Army.

32. United Grand Lodge letter of December 11th 1985, circulated to Grand Officers and lodge secretaries.

33. John Lawrence, *Freemasonry – A religion?* (Kingsway 1987), p.125.

34. *Pillars of Society*, BBC Radio 4, July 1987.

35. Telegraphic address to all masons, June 1987.

36. See note 31.

37. Masons are accused of fostering the old Pelagian heresy of 'salvation by works' in their rituals. Christianity states that man cannot be saved by 'good works' (Ephesians 2:8–9). An example of ritual that encourages masons to trust in themselves for salvation is at Fellow Craft level. The candidate receives his working tools and is told to apply them to his morals. 'In this sense, the Square teaches morality, the Level equality and the Plumb–Rule justness and uprightness of life and actions. Thus by square conduct, level steps and upright intentions we hope to ascend to those immortal mansions whence all goodness emanates.' Grand Lodge have denied this heresy on several occasions. They have no plans to change this ritual.

38. Some ceremonies and rituals focus on a mythical character, Hiram Abiff, supposedly the architect of Solomon's Temple.

39. Anglican Working Group report, p.55.

40. *Manhunt*, *The Christian Man*, and *The Questions Men Ask*, all by Jim Smith (Kingsway 1985, 1986, and 1987).

Chapter 12

1. This description may refer to fresh 'seaside' air, as the gas ozone (O^2) has no smell. One occultist said that it was interesting to note that ectoplasmic mediums have

become noticeably scarce since the introduction of infra-red photography.

2. Shirley MacLaine, *Out on a Limb*, pp.143–147.
3. Brian Inglis, *The Unknown Guest*, 1987.
4. Interview in an Arthur C. Clarke television programme.
5. Extracts from Dr Susan Blackmore's address to the Parapsychology Association at Edinburgh University in 1987.
6. The sample was self-selecting because replies came from 'those who (1) are basically interested in the subject anyway; (2) feel strongly about it one way or another, and (3) have the time and energy to find an envelope and stamp and actually mail the thing off'.
7. Dowsing: Locating latent water or minerals with a divining rod or forked twig.

Chapter 13

1. Billy Graham, *Angels: God's Secret Agents* (Hodder & Stoughton 1975), p.14.
2. J Stafford Wright, 'Psychic Experiences and Phenomena' in *The Christian Parapsychologist*, June 1984, p.194.
3. Ibid, p.193. Sir Alister Hardy explains his theories in *The Spiritual Nature of Man* (Clarendon Press).
4. Ibid, p.189.
5. 'Aims and Objects', *The Quarterly Review of the CFPSS*, flyleaf.
6. Michael Perry, *Psychic Studies – a Christian View*, (Aquarian Press 1984) p.187.
7. Michael Perry, *Deliverance* (SPCK 1987), p.100.
8. Michael Perry, *Psychic Studies*, p.73.

Chapter 14

1. *Gods of the New Age* video, interview with Graham Wilson.
2. *Some Basic Principles*, the Aetherius Society leaflet.

Chapter 15

1. Josh McDowell, *More Evidence That Demands a Verdict*, (Here's Life Publishers).

2. Ibid.

3. One of the greatest Greek astronomers, Hipparchus, catalogued 850 stars which could be detected, using the trigonometry he had invented for the purpose. Astronomers had still only reached a total of 6,000 by the Middle Ages. Plato (428–348 B.C.) was a notable exception.

4. Nelson and Glueck, cited in *Evidence That Demands a Verdict* (Here's Life Publishers), Josh McDowell, p.65.

5. John Stott, article in *The Church of England Newspaper*, April 8, 1988, p.13.

6. Trevor Knight (ed.), *The Search for Faith*, A Young Life Magazine, p.8.

Index